PENGUIN BOOKS

Boring Things Dad Says

Rupert Baxter is a former IT technician turned writer.
He lives in Milton Keynes with his long-suffering
wife and three children.

Beyond writing, Baxter has a passion for garden
landscaping: religiously mowing the lawn every two
weeks, planting cuttings stolen from the local garden
centre, and continuing the ongoing construction of
a water feature that he swears is nearly finished.

Boring Things Dad Says is Baxter's first book. He has
high hopes that it will be a *Sunday Times* bestseller.

Boring Things Dad Says

And what he really means!

RUPERT BAXTER

PENGUIN BOOKS

PENGUIN BOOKS

UK | USA | Canada | Ireland | Australia
India | New Zealand | South Africa

Penguin Books is part of the Penguin Random House group of companies
whose addresses can be found at global.penguinrandomhouse.com

Published in Penguin Books 2024

001

Quote on p. 60 from 'Happiness Is a Warm Gun', recorded
by The Beatles; lyrics by Lennon-McCartney

Quote on p. 73 from the song 'It's the Most Wonderful Time of the
Year', recorded by Andy Williams; lyrics by Eddie Pola/George Wyle

Typeset in 11.5/15.6pt Calluna by Jouve (UK), Milton Keynes
Printed and bound in Great Britain by Clays Ltd, Elcograf S.p.A.

The authorised representative in the EEA is Penguin Random House
Ireland, Morrison Chambers, 32 Nassau Street, Dublin D02 YH68

A CIP catalogue record for this book is
available from the British Library

ISBN: 978-1-804-95335-8

www.greenpenguin.co.uk

Contents

Contents

Introduction

What Dad Says: 'Just do as I say,
   I'm your father.'

What Dad Means: 'I'm winging it here,
   I've no idea what I'm doing.'

Typical Dad Joke: 'Don't call me later,
   call me Dad.'

Dads, like copies of *A Brief History of Time*, are something that everyone seems to have but nobody seems to fully understand. You may be reading this as a very young person still getting to know your dad (in which case be aware there are a couple of bits later on that are slightly fruity and you may need to ask your dad to explain, especially if you like seeing him go bright magenta), or it could be that you've got several decades on the clock trying to understand what he's going on about and have narrowed it down as far as 'It's probably about World War Two'.

   It's not all his fault. There is a tendency amongst

children of all ages, when a dad gets into his stride on a particular topic and really starts laying it on thick, to switch off a bit. Ornithologists say that when a group of birds perches on a telephone wire, while the ones in the middle are completely asleep, those at either end can switch off half their brain to have a bit of a kip while keeping alert for any passing falcons.

In the same way, kids can allocate just enough brain power when their dad is talking so they can chip in with responses – 'Yeah, sorry about that', 'Have you looked under the sink?', 'Alan Shearer, definitely' and so on – to avoid him asking the dreaded question 'Are you even listening to me?' The answer to that question is both yes and no, like a terrified cat filling in a life insurance policy sat next to a poison gas canister in Schrödinger's lab, but that's a more complicated answer than he's looking for.

As a result, some of the nuances in what your dad is saying can get lost. While it might appear on the surface that he's six minutes into a monologue about the daily life of Roman legionaries, what he's really trying to get across is that you should probably try to make a bit more effort to keep your room tidy. There was a point near the beginning, when sandal maintenance was mentioned, that you could have seen the connection he was trying to make (sandals need a lot of looking after, much like a bed frequently needs making, maybe?) but that opportunity has long gone.

Your dad finds you equally baffling. When he asks you how your day was, you often reply in heated tones by asking whether this is Stasi-era East Germany (you've been studying Cold War politics recently, and have had this one loaded up and ready to go for a while) and whether he would like to see your papers?

He was just aware that you had a day, and wondered how it went. That's all.

The key to understanding your dad is less about what he says, because this seldom strays from how much everything costs him, TV shows that were cancelled before you were born, and interesting new routes that cut minutes off his commuting time. It's about what he actually means when he says things.

You've seen this in action with your mum's interactions with your dad. Don't believe me?

Fine.

What does 'fine' mean, when said to your dad? It can mean anything from 'I don't care if you turn the TV over, I'm not watching it anyway' or 'I don't have the energy to continue this argument so I'm going to let you think you won so it can be over', all the way up to 'What you just said might see you sleeping in the garage for the next six months unless you make a swift and elegant dismount right this very second'.

It's not about the word 'fine'; it's about the context that surrounds it. Similarly, you need to listen not just to what your dad says but the context in which he says it. If he asks you whether you remembered to renew your passport while you're sat in his living room and he's halfway through a tirade about how useless the DVLA are, it's a harmless question prompted by a misfiring neuron concerned with the uselessness of officialdom in general. If he asks you in the departures lounge of Heathrow while surrounded by the rest of your family, you may be advised to just run away and never look back.

And it's not as if dads are difficult beings to maintain. Most of them take less looking after than a cactus, and like cactuses (cacti? The jury is out) are spiky, show little signs of growth and have a preference to bask in hot weather.

Keep them fed and watered, surreptitiously throw out their underwear when the hole-to-cloth ratio tips over 50 per cent, buy them a house-brick-sized book on Tudor history for their birthday, and dads basically look after themselves. What your dad desires above all else is a quiet life, which might seem paradoxical when he's shouting at the universe in general because a cricketer halfway across the world just dropped a small red ball – or because a light bulb he bought when Steps were still an ongoing pop concern has had the audacity to stop working.

Think of all the times you had a quieter life thanks to the intervention of your dad. He paid for the repair of that window before your mum found out what had happened. He drove you away from a painful break-up with a car full of your stuff and turned the radio up to muffle any crying. He was, when it mattered, there.

What this book aims to do is to give you pointers of What Dad Says versus What Dad Means in a number of key stages throughout your life. Not all scenarios are covered, of course. To comprehensively explain what your dad actually means in every given situation would require the kind of series of books they advertise on TV channels in the mid-500s, where you get the first volume free along with a ballpoint pen and subsequent volumes cost £39.99 – yes, that's right, just £39.99 – from now until the end of recorded time.

Depending on your age, you may have already experienced some of the situations the book covers and have walked away from them either shaking your head, letting out a slow, heavy sigh of exasperation or waving your hands about in the air shouting, 'God, you're so irritating, I can't believe we're even related'. These reactions are not age-reliant and you can find yourself taking the path of quiet tolerance as a teenager or slamming the door to your room and playing very loud music about how nobody understands you when you're in your forties. You're never too old for a good tantrum.

Equally, there may be sections covering situations you have yet to experience. The thought of having children yourself, when you currently struggle to look after the school hamster during summer holidays (hamsters are creation's greatest mistakes and have the life expectancy of an ice cream in a steelworks factory, so don't feel too bad about it if it does go paws-up on your watch), might be a daunting one but hopefully forewarned is forearmed if or when that day comes. Additional advice like 'you *will* be pooped on' and 'get used to everything smelling of vomit' is probably more information than younger readers are ready for, so let's draw a veil over all that.

Oscar Wilde said that children 'begin by loving their parents; as they grow older they judge them; sometimes they forgive them'. Far be it from me to give advice to one of history's greatest writers but he could have added that 'at no point in the process do they ever really understand them'. No matter how far along Oscar's journey you are, there will be something in this book for you, either to look back on and wish you had done differently or to provide little nuggets of ammunition in your back pocket for when they arise.

Think of it as a handbook for your dad. But unlike when your dad buys flat-pack furniture, this is a handbook you will actually read.

The Breakfast Table

What Dad Says: 'So, what's everyone up
to today?'

What Dad Means: 'I want to put off
thinking about what I'm doing
today for as long as possible.'

Typical Dad Joke: 'Shredded Wheat? I bet
you're not having three.' (This joke refers
to a slogan whose origins have been lost
in the deepest archives of history.)

Your dad will tell you that breakfast is the most
important meal of the day. This seems doubtful when
you compare his reaction of a morning to a plate of
lukewarm toast and his reaction on a Friday night when
a moped driver turns up at the front door with a dozen
cartons of Indian food and a four-pack of Cobra lager.
If he opened those cartons and found cornflakes inside,
it's very possible he might break down and start crying.
Indeed, when compared to most other meals – fish and

chips by the seaside, a Sunday roast in a country pub and so on – breakfast pales in comparison.

Only two types of breakfast pique the interest of the average dad. One is a massive fry-up to stave off the symptoms of a hangover, washed down with enough tea to drown a moose. Your dad will assure you there are sound medical reasons why this breakfast is the best remedy for a night on the beers, mentioning the toxin-absorbent properties of protein strands, the anti-oxidant content of grilled tomatoes, and the recent research into the health benefits of fried bread.

The other breakfast of interest is the sheer majesty of a hotel all-you-can-eat buffet on holiday. The buffet energises your dad's ingenuity like few other tasks. It is, he will tell you, a three-course meal, rather than the single visit to pick up cereal and a bit of fruit that amateurs like your mum will settle for. The Hobbits knew what they were on about when it came to breakfast, your dad feels.

The first course involves as close to a Full English as the Spanish/Greek/Turkish caterers can provide. Well aware of dad-preferences, most will lay out a vast tureen of baked beans – a lukewarm orange cauldron where the juice/bean ratio leans dangerously towards the juice, requiring patient spoon-draining techniques. Eggs will be present. Scrambled eggs for certain, cooked to a consistency where they could be firmly pressed into a serviceable squash ball. There may also be fried eggs, and your dad will consider the holiday a success if he manages to get one fresh enough that the yolk still has dippy qualities.

There will also be something the hotel has the sheer audacity to call bacon but might be better described as 'flat strips of pig the colour of a strangulated hernia and the texture of a shoelace'. This will not stop it from being added to your dad's plate. Hash browns will suffice in the absence of chips, and he's perfectly happy to stand for fifteen minutes with a queue behind him like it's the January sales while the conveyor-belt toaster turns a small piece of bread, apparently slathered in factor 50 sun cream, one Pantone shade browner than when it went in.

The second course is a free-for-all delicatessen nightmare. Whatever sliced cheeses, hams, pickles, olives, dips, breadsticks, and unrecognisable items that could be goat meat or could be a napkin will be piled high and methodically sampled, with your dad occasionally pulling a disgusted face and waving a ribbon of animal under your nose, asking if you want to try a piece. This, he will claim, is all part of sampling the local culture – in lieu of going to look at those ancient ruins they mentioned in the guidebook.

Once this has been washed down with orange juice ('orange' in the singular rather than the plural is apt here, given how diluted it is) served in a glass of the size typically reserved for shots of Sambuca, it's time for dessert.

What Dad Says: 'There's always room for dessert!'

What Dad Means: 'I could've bought a Ferrari for the price of this all-inclusive, I'm getting my money's worth.'

Buffets will usually have a selection of small pastries, one of which will be placed onto a plate and consumed with a tiny cup of jet-black coffee by the more sophisticated continental guests at the hotel. Your dad will pile them onto his plate like it's a skip behind a patisserie, and then go off to see if they have any ice cream to go with it. A dad's buffet breakfast dessert is basically any food in the room with a sugar content higher than water.

This is why dads like sitting by the pool all morning as they doze off in the vicinity of a paperback book. They need time to digest a meal of such magnitude, like a python basking in the Argentinian sun with a belly full of wild pig.

Back home, the importance of breakfast for your dad is to make sure you're sufficiently energised at school to pay attention and avoid the kind of behaviour – hangry outbursts, dozing off at your desks and so on – that will require him to make an appointment to see your teachers.

Another function it fulfils is to create a background noise until his second cup of coffee kicks in and he can steel himself to leave the house and go to work. Work will have several synonyms depending on how well things are going for your dad. 'The old grindstone' means that while he's not exactly Chief Executive of the Fun Factory, he's also not obsessively refreshing the page on the human resources website that tells him how much his pension would be worth if he cashed it out tomorrow. 'That (expletive) place' is a bad sign, clearly – as is the more brusque 'Right. Back later', as this suggests your dad can't even bring himself to acknowledge that a place called 'work' exists and he is expected to keep going back to it.

While nobody in your family wants to see your dad dread the idea of going to his job, if he dashes out of the house with a round of toast in his hand and a song on his lips half an hour before he needs to leave, questions may be asked about why he's so keen to sit in traffic for an hour to get to a place that makes injected plastic mouldings, rather than spend a second longer with his family. One day you may even be bored enough to ask him what injected plastic mouldings actually are.

What Dad Says: 'Have you done
your homework?'

What Dad Means: 'What have you forgotten
to tell me you need for school?'

In the same way you're vaguely aware that your dad earns a living doing something with plastic, injections and some kind of mould, he is aware that your school life involves things that occasionally require his attention, permission or payment.

He will periodically have a progress report card placed in front of him, to let the school inform your dad what a genius/plodder/complete moron (delete as appropriate) he's raising. Your school may also ask for parental permission for part of your education, but given the fact very few educational establishments teach shark fishing or base jumping, his signature should probably be a formality. All they want to do is make a classroom of teenagers wish they were anywhere else on the planet than sat listening to a teacher (who feels exactly the same way) talk haltingly about the human reproductive system.

Sometimes the school will need money from your dad. This is unlikely to be a large amount, unless you go to the kind of school that has its own moat keeper, polo fields, sommelier, and a crest that features a knight resplendent, stepping on the throat of a peasant passant, with crossed hockey sticks.

No sum of money is so small that your dad will fail to ask what they are trying to gouge out of him now, whether it's really necessary for you to pass your exams, how much it can possibly cost to teach kids how to read and write these days, and what, actually, does he pay taxes for? Like the safety demonstration on an airplane, this is a performance you've seen many times before and have to sit through before you can proceed. It also features just as many extravagant arm gestures.

What Dad Says: 'I'm off, don't do
    anything I wouldn't do.'

What Dad Means: 'I'm going to spend a
    third of my day sitting with people I've
    no choice about socialising with, doing
    something I'd rather not do, while
    somebody watches me and tells me off if I
    don't do it properly. You're going to school.
    You'll be doing exactly what I'm doing.'

Although breakfast usually ends with a mass exodus from the house, working from home has become increasingly common and has changed the dynamic of the breakfast table with your dad. Previously, he had the chance to berate everybody for being part-timers because he had to leave before they did to get to work (ignoring the fact that his workplace being several miles away was not your fault and the fact your school was just around the corner was because that's kind of how local schools work).

Working from home (and your dad will insist on emphasising that just because he's at home he is still *working*, thank you very much) means your dad will now chivvy everybody out of the house as soon as breakfast is finished, because he can't properly concentrate until he has the place to himself.

You have your suspicions. The sofa is looking more . . . slept on these days. The Xbox controller isn't always where you left it the day before. And couriers leave 'We called but you weren't at home' cards a lot more than they used to, which was frequent enough to begin with even when you were sat in the living room watching them sprint away from your doorstep, tossing the calling card over their shoulder into the recycling bin.

Ultimately, it doesn't really matter whether your dad skives a bit when working from home. You'd do the same if you were allowed to do school from home, and at least if he's in the house, nobody will get angry with him when he starts absent-mindedly scratching his backside as he tries to remember why he went into the kitchen.

The Birthday Party

What Dad Says: 'You're getting a bit old
  for birthday parties, aren't you?'

What Dad Means: 'Thirty screaming kids
  running about my house, are you insane?'

Typical Dad Joke: (Holds up a straight balloon)
  'Here, I made a snake.'

When you think of birthday parties, you probably think of presents, having fun with your friends and eating far too much cake. If 'far too much cake' is actually a thing, of course – the scientific community is still disputing the very existence of this phenomenon.

For this reason, you may find the dad reaction to birthday parties rather puzzling. Observe the furrowed brow, the shortness of both breath and temper, the distracted air of somebody who is not in the midst of a disaster but has definitely just received a text telling him to expect one somewhere between the hours of 9 a.m. and 5 p.m.

This is because birthday parties require a dad to:

- Remember Stuff
- Go Places
- Meet People

None of which he would do himself given the choice. Carrying out one of these duties can test the resources of even the most resilient dad, but combining all three can be like asking him to simultaneously pat his head, rub his stomach and recite the whole of *Hamlet*, backwards.

If we break down the challenges a birthday party can throw up ('throwing up' being one of them, given the presence of toddlers and the excess consumption of cake previously mentioned) it might make the tell-tale signs of stress easier to spot.

REMEMBER STUFF

What Dad Says: 'It's Stephen's birthday party this Saturday, isn't it?'

What Dad Means: 'The Post-it note about this party that has been on the fridge for the last two months may as well contain the secret recipe for Coca-Cola for all the attention I've paid to it.'

This is not the straightforward request for information it might appear at first glance. Dad is not just asking whether Stephen's party is, in fact, on Saturday. Unspoken in the question is the hope that maybe, without his knowledge and by some blessed miracle, the party has been cancelled and his Saturday can be the sofa-based day of television, snacks and horizontality he would prefer.

Perhaps Stephen and his whole family have suddenly packed up and moved to a small farm in Costa Rica in the dead of night. Maybe Stephen's parents have realised that his birthday was actually last month and they've been getting the date wrong all these years. Maybe Stephen isn't the seven-year-old that goes to school with your little brother, like everyone thought, and has been arrested with a lunchbox full of state secrets as a Russian spy with a growth-hormone problem.

Anything is possible.

Also implicit in Dad's question is whether his presence is still required. Your mum could take the day off work to drive everyone there, perhaps? He knows better than to ask questions like this directly, as evidenced by the Great Silence of September 2023, hence the vagueness of the phrasing. But everyone could get on three buses across town to get there rather than him driving them, couldn't they? It'd be an adventure.

Once it's been made clear that yes, a person called

Stephen still exists, and yes, he is still expecting all his friends to arrive at his house this Saturday, and no, he hasn't changed his religion to Jehovah's Witness and stopped celebrating birthdays altogether, there will be other stuff to remember.

What Dad Says: 'What present did
     we end up buying him?'

What Dad Means: 'I know for a fact that I didn't
     buy Stephen, a kid I vaguely know as a small
     mass of snot and freckles, a birthday present,
     given the difficulty I have remembering
     to buy gifts for my immediate family.'

What he wants to know is what present was bought so he doesn't look as surprised as Stephen does when it gets unwrapped. This also lets him know how much money was spent on somebody else's child. Money that could have been better spent on any number of items your dad would quite like for himself.

Dad might not be the best person in the world at mental arithmetic, but he can work out in an instant what fraction of an Xbox game, book on World War Two history or bottle of Merlot Stephen's gift has just denied him from enjoying. 'Happy birthday, Stephen. I hope you like one-third of the new *Call of Duty*.'

What Dad Says: 'What time do
we need to head off?'

What Dad Means: 'I have no idea when
the invite said to arrive, how long we're
expected to stay when we get there or
what postcode Stephen even lives in.'

Getting ready to leave for the party will take place
in stages, starting early in the morning with vague
mentions from Dad about 'that damned party we're all
being dragged to'. He will not notice that while he feels
he is being dragged along like a dog refusing to go for
a walk, the prospect of the party has had your little
brother bouncing off the walls like a subatomic particle
in the Large Hadron Collider since Tuesday.

There will be a crescendo of irritation as the day
goes on, with Dad needing to make sure everybody is
showered and has eaten breakfast, so when they arrive
they don't attack the party buffet like a pack of starv-
ing raccoons, and that everybody is wearing the correct
number of shoes (preferably both of the same make
and model).

Dad will have been informed that his usual Saturday clothing will not be deemed acceptable, as it is not
a fancy-dress party and he is not allowed to arrive looking like a scarecrow. His grumbling about having to

shave and put on a clean shirt will not go unnoticed by your little brother as he complains about being forced into a similarly strict hygiene routine that demands he brush all his teeth.

The gift and birthday card (signed by the whole family, including Dad's heartwarming personalised message 'Happy Birthday, Stephen') will have been left next to the front door with the car keys on top of them, to minimise the risk of them being forgotten in the rush to leave, given that any outing of this nature will always commence at the last possible moment.

Once Dad has left the house with the gift, the card and, if he has been paying attention, the correct number of kids, the last thing he needs to remember is the address he's driving to so he can put it into the car's satnav.

What Dad Says: 'Oh, so that's where Stephen lives, is it?'

What Dad Means: 'I wouldn't ordinarily drive through that part of town at ninety miles an hour in an armoured truck with a police escort. Wind up all the windows and keep your valuables in your pocket.'

or

'I couldn't afford to buy a shed in that part of town, let alone a house. The present we bought Stephen is going to look sarcastically cheap, and I now think I should've worn a shirt that was both clean *and* free of holes.'

Despite all outward signs to the contrary, Dad actually likes where he lives. He even likes the people who live there, although he'd never say this out loud. He knows where 99 per cent of everything is – the 1 per cent exception being whatever he's looking for at any given moment – he can walk around in his pants without being arrested, and he feels safe there when he's not being asked to leave it to Go Places and Meet People.

But he will always compare your house to the houses of other dads he encounters and he will rank it in a league table that exists entirely inside his own mind. To him, your house is probably a respectable mid-table house that can hold its head up when compared with others while also never being able to compete with the fancy title-winning houses of other dads who can afford luxuries like jacuzzis, en-suite bathrooms, and door handles that don't fall off every six months.

An occasion like a birthday party, where your dad has to go to another dad's house for the first time, is an away fixture with a team he's never competed against before. He will give himself a pep talk in the car before setting off, reminding himself that at the end of the day his house gives it 110 per cent every week, and he's proud of all of its achievements like the roof not leaking and the bathroom mould being under control – and if the other dad's house is victorious, then he probably did it by cheating on his taxes or something.

GO PLACES

What Dad Says: 'Can we have the radio on? I need to hear the traffic reports.'

What Dad Means: 'If I have to listen to the *Moana* soundtrack one more time I'm going to steer this car into oncoming traffic.'

Car journeys with Dad can be fraught. Tensions can run high with him when you have an entire house to dilute the hot soup of annoyance your family can make together. Now imagine bottling that soup up in a small flask and propelling it at high speed past other soup flasks of irritation coming in the opposite direction. Your dad needs something to help defuse the tension, and an ex-wrestler singing about how great his cartoon alter-ego is won't do it.

You are aware that the radio station Dad picks in order to listen to the traffic reports is not a news channel nor a local radio station but rather a station that specialises in the music that came out when he was between the ages of thirteen and twenty-five (or, if he is much older, music that came out in about 1846 that you can't even hum along to). It will have a name like 'Drivetime Classic Remember When You Used to Have Hair FM'. This is not a coincidence.

When your dad was younger, way back in the distant mists of time, he found Going Places to be an enjoyable activity. He could be going somewhere he actually wanted to go to, like a music festival, or a party where the jelly came from the freezer in shot glasses and the coats in the bedroom sometimes had something underneath them that was more exciting than 'more coats'.

Of course, he wouldn't swap his current life for that life. Staying awake past 11 p.m. sounds frankly exhausting to him, and the last time he dabbled in drugs was when he changed his brand of deep heat for when his back goes into spasm after a game of five-a-side. But he enjoys listening to the songs his dad said were just a noise (and, in turn, your dad's dad loved songs that *his* dad said were just a noise. No doubt half a million years ago there was a caveman, at the grand old age of thirty-six, telling his kid that in his day they used to make proper music by banging rocks together rather than this new-fangled stick-banging rubbish).

Your journey will be punctuated by your dad occasionally turning the radio up, twisting in his seat and telling you that this is a proper tune right here. He may call it a banger. He may even air-drum with his fingers on the steering wheel. He may, if you're very unlucky, attempt to sing along.

When this happens, just console yourself with the knowledge that there has never been a recorded case of somebody actually cringing themselves inside out.

What Dad Says: 'Look at this idiot.'

What Dad Means: 'JESUS £%$^ING @£&$^@ YOU PIECE OF ^@@* I WILL &@^£ YOUR *&@^ING @&£^$^ OFF!'

Your dad is an excellent driver. It's a little-known fact that every dad is an excellent driver. Ask any driving instructor whether they've ever had to fail somebody on their test and they will say, 'Of course, all the time, we're very strict about standards, you know.' Ask them if any of those failed tests were dads and they will look at you with disdain and disbelief, as if you have just asked them whether they've ever tried to drive an octopus through a shopping centre. 'Don't be ridiculous,' they will say, drawing the conversation to a brusque finish. 'I would entrust every dad behind the wheel of a car with my life.'

This is, of course, nonsense.

Every dad *thinks* they are an expert driver. They pride themselves on their ability to steer their decade-old Honda through the streets of your hometown like Nigel Mansell/Michael Schumacher/Lewis Hamilton (depending on their age) smoothly rounding the last corner of Silverstone.

You can insult their appearance, their personal hygiene, even their taste in films (although you should avoid telling them that *Goodfellas* is rubbish unless you have two hours to spare hearing why you're wrong). But tell them they can't parallel park to save their lives and you'd better start browsing the local orphanages for vacant beds.

Empirical evidence isn't in your dad's favour. The other cars on the road, the ones who must have won their driving licence in a raffle, are often driven by other dads. You've been in the car with your dad when another dad in another car has angrily honked his horn at your dad for some apparent foul play. But your dad is a great driver, so the fault must be with that other dad in that other car. But all dads are great drivers, so . . .

It's the kind of paradox that made Greek philosophers

throw their hands up in despair and decide to sit in a tree for thirty years.

Another paradox of being in the car with your dad is that Swearing Is Bad Except When It Isn't. From the moment you shouted the word 'BUMS' as a toddler you've been told in solemn tones, more disappointed than upset, that foul language just isn't on. You know better than this, as it's explained to you.

Until your dad has experienced one too many inconsiderate drivers in a row and – 'Look at this idiot' – lets somebody out of a side road who doesn't thank him, and he morphs into a bar full of sailors on shore leave simultaneously stubbing their toes. You will hear words you've never heard before, describing parts of the body you didn't know existed.

This is quickly forgotten and the default rule – Swearing Is Bad – is restored. If you dare to say anything stronger than 'crikey' you will get the lecture from this potty-tongued dad as if butter wouldn't melt in his sewer of a mouth. The dream scenario is receiving this lecture in heavy traffic. Try saying a rude word during a car journey and sitting back to have the Swearing Is Bad lecture suddenly interrupted.

'You're a clever kid, you have a good vocabulary. You don't need to swear to get your p . . . WHAT ARE YOU PLAYING AT YOU F£%\$£&^ STUPID £&^\$H OF £^%@.'

The reason Swearing Is Bad Except When It Isn't is that the other driver could have killed everyone with their recklessness, so it was a natural expression of protectiveness from your dad, who loves you so much that he sometimes lets a few bad words slip out by mistake.

If you want to hear a few more bad words, try telling your dad his three-point turns have more points than a basketball game.

What Dad Says: 'Okay, we're here, now don't go making a show of me in front of everyone.'

What Dad Means: 'Please don't behave in front of strangers the way you do at home.'

Nobody knows how anybody else actually behaves. This is something your dad is aware of and is something he is trying to get you to understand.

You know this in a subconscious way growing up, immediately turning into a wild savage the second a teacher leaves the classroom and a stuttering imbecile the second that person you fancy starts talking to you. There's the version of you immediately before asking your dad if you can stay out until 10 p.m. and the version of you immediately after being told you absolutely cannot stay out until all hours of the night.

But in addition to this, there's an At Home version of you, your dad, and anyone else in the household that is not for public consumption. For instance, somebody may have the nickname of Sir Fartsalot around the house, but in front of strangers it's considered polite to call them by the same name the vicar did at their christening (unless you have very quirky parents and a very understanding vicar and that is your actual name).

If you want to see how true this is, inform your dad that you forgot to tell him that a friend of his said they would be coming round to visit and are due in the next half hour. Then stand well back.

The house you see every day of the week becomes a strange and pristine environment. The carpet becomes visible once more from under mountains of clothes, toys, books and half-eaten slices of toast. Dishes are no longer left in the sink 'to give them a soak'. The TV is turned down to a whisper, for reasons that are never and will never be explained to you.

And when you go into Stephen's house for the birthday party, you aren't actually going into Stephen's house. You're going into a version of Stephen's house that his dad isn't embarrassed by the world seeing and Stephen himself probably barely recognises, because it has been tidied to within an inch of his life to avoid anybody making a show of Stephen's dad.

MEET PEOPLE

What Dad Says: 'Henry, isn't it?
   Thanks for inviting us.'

What Dad Means: 'Neither of us wants to be
   here, Henry, so let's just get through this, eh?'

Your dad will make a point of referring to Stephen's
dad by name half a dozen times in the first fifteen minutes after arriving. This is not because he thinks Henry
is such a brilliant name he can't stop saying it, but
because if he doesn't he will completely forget it and
have to fall back on referring to him as 'Stephen's dad'.

This would appear rude to Stephen's dad – sorry,
Henry. Henry has invited your dad into his home,
Henry is about to watch your dad's kids eat Taylor
Swift's annual concert catering budget in party food,
and there's a fair chance one of you will leave a stain
on Henry's sofa that never quite fades. The least your
dad can do is remember his name.

The politeness of the greeting between your dad
and . . . Henry is more strained than a waistband on
Boxing Day. If you think your dad has had a stressful
morning getting everybody from your house to here,
compared to Henry's morning it's been like two weeks
in the Maldives.

Henry is a dad who has been asked a hundred questions in the last few days, none of which he knows the answer to, cares about or understands the consequences of getting wrong. Pass The Parcel or Musical Chairs? Face painting or not? Are any of the kids vegan? Do we give the kids gift bags when they arrive or leave? Or at all? Are you listening to any of this? Why are you crying? What do you mean can you just go to the pub for an hour?

Your dad calculated the cost of Stephen's gift in fractions of an Xbox game. Henry has calculated the cost of this party, plus the mound of birthday gifts piled in the corner like an extravagant temple of debt, in fractions of a new car.

Henry has been blowing up balloons since 7 a.m. and his lungs now feel like he's been chain-smoking burning tyres. Henry has to clear all this away once your dad and all the other dads have stayed long enough to be polite plus twenty minutes (it's a precise figure that comes with years of dad practice) and gone home. Henry has two other kids and has to do this once every four months for the next decade or so.

Henry is really, really tired.

What Dad Says: 'You should play with
    Sammy more often, he's a nice kid.'

What Dad Means: 'Sammy's parents are loaded
and his dad has a recreation room with
Sky Sports and a TV the size of a snooker
table. He also has a snooker table.'

Your dad understands that socialising with other dads is an unavoidable part of dad life, like watching his kids be terrible at sport while cheering or having to make a prior appointment to use the bathroom of a morning. And since this has to be the case, then he will encourage you to make friends with kids whose dads make the whole thing as painless as possible.

There will be the Platonic ideal of a dad out there for your dad to befriend. One that won't start conversations about sports your dad doesn't watch and has always felt inadequate about not being able to play. A dad who doesn't enjoy high-brow cultural activities your dad doesn't understand because he prefers watching Netflix series about bad people doing awful things then getting caught. A dad who has a bar in his house. The dream dad.

If you look closely, you will see your dad working the room at a birthday party to try to find the dream dad. He will also be in constant motion to avoid being roped into helping with any of the activities that Stephen doesn't want to join in with because they're getting in between him and opening that stack of presents.

A birthday party is a perfect opportunity to see what dad opportunities are out there and gently nudge friendships in the right direction accordingly. If you ever wondered why your dad kept telling you to invite that boring kid who smelled weird over to play and the kid in question turned up in a BMW driven by a mum who looked like one of Leonardo DiCaprio's exes, now you know why.

What Dad Says: 'We'd better go,
   he's getting a bit tired.'

What Dad Means: 'I'd better go,
   I'm getting a bit tired.'

Your little brother could be doing circuits of the house with flames shooting from his feet – a tiny sticky blur of food additives and shouting – but when your dad has decided he's done his duty and stayed long enough, he will wrestle the little dervish back into the car, insisting that he'll be fast asleep within minutes.

Your dad needs to build up to this moment. Just blurting it out can look rude, and he doesn't want to look rude in front of that very promising dad he just met who mentioned that he has a villa in Portugal he lets his friends use from time to time.

He may pat his pockets distractedly, making sure he has his keys, wallet and half a dozen stolen packs of Haribo he's going to eat later, when everyone else has gone to bed. Variations on 'Well, it's been lovely catching up with you' will be said to all the parents present, even the ones he didn't speak to, as well as the dad who's really into yoga and once offered to teach your dad how to do the Recumbent Antelope pose to help with his back pain.

Your dad will thank Henry once more for inviting him, although Henry has been nipping into the bathroom for the last hour to take sneaky belts of whisky from his hip flask to numb the pain, and is currently trying to assemble Stephen's new pedal car with all the glassy-eyed manual dexterity of a sack full of mismatched gloves.

It's a gradual process that takes time, and must be carefully calibrated to make sure it can be completed without looking rushed, to ensure there's enough time to round up everybody and get them back into the car amidst their howls of complaint – and enough time to miss the early evening traffic so your dad can be back at home in front of Ant & Dec on the TV, which is all he wanted from this Saturday in the first place.

What Dad Says: 'Well, that was fun.'

What Dad Means: '(Sigh).'

In a universe plagued on all sides with injustice, hardship and woe, your dad finds himself alone in a pinnacle of suffering when he realises, two minutes after backside makes contact with sofa, that he drank the last beer in the fridge last night and the corner shop closed ten minutes ago.

What Dad Says: 'That's a shame.'

What Dad Means: 'Arrgghhhhhhhh.'

The Parents' Evening

What Dad Says: 'Here's where we find
   out what you've really been up to.'

What Dad Means: 'If you've not set fire
   to anything or anyone, I'm fine with
   you failing Religious Studies.'

Typical Dad Joke: 'Better not shave or
   they'll think I'm one of the pupils!'

Your dad treats your academic progress in much the
same way he treats his car. If none of the warning
lights start flashing on the dashboard, he assumes the
car must be fine, and if none of your school reports
include phrases like 'immediate suspension', 'serious
concerns' or 'CID have been informed', he assumes
you're doing okay at school.

But a parents' evening is the equivalent of the mech-
anic opening the car bonnet and pointing at things in
the engine while your dad stands next to them nodding along as if he has any idea what they're talking

about. A discussion about the fuel injection system causing rough idling below twenty thousand revs will be met with the same glassy stare as when your English teacher tells him you're struggling with subjunctive clauses.

(Nobody will admit this – not your teachers, not university English professors, not even the most successful authors in the world – but nobody knows what a subjunctive clause actually is, what it looks like or what it does. Stand up in class and say in a confident-enough tone that a subjunctive clause is Santa's younger brother, and nobody will dare contradict you for fear of looking stupid.)

You may view the approach of a parents' evening with dread, but if it's any consolation, so does your dad. You may be keen to point out that pupils aren't required to come along to a parents' evening, but all this will do is raise the faint hope in your dad's mind that he isn't technically required to attend either. This is all in vain, though. You both have to attend, so you may as well make peace with the fact.

The timing of a parents' evening is vital but is sadly completely outside of your control. You could hit a rich academic vein without one on the horizon, and suddenly start failing every subject just as the next one comes along. Such is life.

Equally, they could schedule the parents' evening on the same day your dad's team is in a cup quarter-final or when he usually goes to the pub quiz. Equally outside of your control – but the constant low-level grumbling from your dad leading up to the big day will suggest that in some deep, imperceptible way, this was entirely your fault.

When you're older, a piece of sound relationship advice is to get your partner something nice every now and then for no reason at all. The reason for this is two-fold. First, it shows that you love, respect and care for them. Second, when you screw up (and you will), you can defend the small bunch of flowers/four-pack of fancy beers/two weeks' all-inclusive holiday to Cancún (depending on the nature and the enormity of the screw-up) that accompanies your apology by truthfully saying you don't just buy them things when you're in trouble.

In the same way, it's no good being nice to your dad mere days before the parents' evening. He's had enough bunches of garage-forecourt apology flowers thrown back at him to spot that tactic. If you think you're going to need to soften him up before the big night, you'd better plan weeks in advance – even if that means hours of garden maintenance, dishwasher-loading, and listening to 'Peg' while being told why Steely Dan were the best band ever.

What Dad Says: 'So, which teacher
  should we speak to first?'

What Dad Means: 'Which class are you failing
  the most? Let's get it out of the way.'

The parents' evening often takes place in the school gymnasium. This is because it's the one room in the school big enough to accommodate all the teachers, pupils and parents at tables far enough away from each other that your dad doesn't overhear how incredibly thick everyone else in your class is, or how you are one of the incredibly thick ones compared to the child genius at the next desk.

The gymnasium is also used for reasons of psycho-geography. The theory of psychogeography states that a particular place or building can influence the emotions and experiences of the people in the vicinity. More-experimental psychogeographers suggest that the building itself can absorb the experiences and emotions of people over the years and feed it back to people at a later time.

So, if you want to pick a place where kids hate every second they're there and wish the ground would swallow them up while disappointed adults look on, there's no more appropriate place than a school gymnasium.

Your dad will scan the room to see which tables

have the biggest queues, so he can get the evening wrapped up as quickly as possible – maybe even in time to see the second half of the match. In this respect, a parents' evening is a bit like a comic convention where they have people signing memorabilia.

The queue length equates to how seriously you, your dad or even (if they're being entirely honest) the teacher takes the subject in question. The table for Maths will be like the Peter Capaldi table at a *Doctor Who* convention. You'd better go to the toilet before you join the back of that beast of a line.

The Drama table, on the other hand, will be like the Bloke Who Played a Cyberman Back in 1988 table. While the performing arts are a fine and noble pursuit, as far as your dad – and pretty much every other dad in the room – is concerned, no employer is going to be scanning your CV to see how good you are at pretending to be a tree.

The exception to this rule is the Hot Teacher table. Every school has a Hot Teacher, with sliding scales of hotness relative to the rest of the teaching staff. In a school lacking in hotness, Hot Teacher status can be conferred on a member of staff if their appearance doesn't frighten livestock and they have more than three of their own teeth. Most schools also have a Thinks They're the Hot Teacher member of staff, who assumes the older pupils are flirting with them and is often replaced at a moment's notice by a substitute teacher for reasons that are never explained to the pupils.

The Hot Teacher table could be discussing how well pupils are doing at tying their shoelaces or sitting still during school assembly, but they will still have a steady stream of parents (half of whom are visibly angry at how long they've been sat there) listening raptly to every word.

When you sit down at one of the main tables like History (Sophie Aldred – worth speaking to but not A division) or English (David Tennant – no mucking about here, this is the important stuff), your dad will adopt his Paying Attention face, usually reserved for when your mum is telling him news about her side of the family, or a builder is explaining why a new garden fence will actually need a bulldozer hiring, will take two weeks and will mean you're not going on holiday this year.

When the teacher explains in graphic detail how badly you're doing and your dad needs to maintain his Paying Attention face rather than going nuclear, he'll wish he spent more time at the Drama table asking for acting tips.

What Dad Says: 'What can we be doing
at home to help them catch up?'

What Dad Means: 'How much is a tutor going to cost?'

The teachers will explain where you're going wrong and what needs to be done to rectify the situation. The problem with this is it's likely your dad will have forgotten 97.4 per cent of everything they taught him in school when he was your age, and he'll be damned if he's going to learn it all over again just so you can get a C in Geography.

When he says things like 'Is "I before E except after C" still a thing?' or '*La plage est une bibliothèque avec du fromage bleu, s'il vous plaît* – pretty sure that's right', you can see your 5 grades rapidly becoming 4 grades with his intervention.

Instead of focusing on academic specifics to improve your grades, your dad will instead lean on concepts like application, hard work and the pulling up of socks. Confiscation of game consoles will be mooted, mobile phone usage will be monitored, and there may even be talk of grounding (even though your dad no more wants to spend an evening with you sulking around the house than you do).

Anything to avoid him having to grapple with algebra, really.

You can also tell how badly you're doing by how much your dad leaps on any positive comments from your teachers. 'Interacts well with others' is the kind of thing a cat sanctuary mentions when trying to off-load a fourteen-year-old tabby with kidney problems, but in this context your dad will take praise where he can find it. Punctuality, good attendance, always has correct uniform/P E kit/a pen . . . You can't be an absolute washout with comments like that, surely?

What Dad Says: 'We'll talk about
   this when we get home.'

What Dad Means: 'I'm out of my depth
   and need time to think of something.'

The reason for all of this is that your dad can vividly remember being sat where you are now, hearing the same kinds of failings being discussed and feeling the burning-hot glow of disappointment from all the adults concerned.

He remembers feeling like he was trying his best and everyone was out to get him. He remembers how hard it was just to get through the day avoiding bullying, peer pressure, the fear of Talking to Somebody You Fancy, and not feeling cool enough or popular enough or even just tall enough.

He'd have done school differently if he knew then what he knows now, but that's impossible, so the only option he has left is to try to make sure you don't make the same mistakes.

But making mistakes is the whole point of growing up – just look at any adult who spent their whole childhood being told they were brilliant and could do no wrong and grew up to be president, to take an example entirely at random – so he knows you have to make your own mistakes, and he has to tell you off for them so you'll learn from them, and he has to sit there while you make even more mistakes.

And sometimes he has to do that while sitting in a gymnasium.

The Music Gig

What Dad Says: 'I love all kinds of music,
I've got really eclectic taste.'

What Dad Means: 'Except that rubbish you're
listening to, apparently just to annoy me.'

Typical Dad Joke: 'Rap, is it? Is that
with a silent C, is it?'

Music is very important to dads, as it takes them back
to when they were teenagers and they used to spend
their days looking scruffy, moaning about how unfair
everything was, and generally embarrassing the rest
of their family. This is not a million miles away from
how they behave now, of course, but the scruffy long
hair has been replaced by a cut from the £10 barber
next to Timpson, the unfairness of not being allowed
to paint their room black is now the unfairness of
having to spend the whole of Sunday at IKEA, and
they embarrass the whole family with how cool they

think they are when they actually aren't. Some things never change.

Dads will tell you that when they were your age, the charts were full of Proper Music.

What Dad Says: 'When I was your age,
   the charts were full of Proper Music.'

What Dad Means: 'New music scares
   me in a way involving mortality
   that I can't quite explain.'

Proper Music can be identified in general terms. Typically it will be a song of about four minutes long, played by guitarists and a drummer (with a keyboard player thrown in if the band are trying to 'expand their sound'), and the band members will look as if they smell like the carpet in a Wetherspoons.

All visible light can be divided into three primary colours – red, blue and yellow – and Proper Music songs can be divided into four primary topics – drinking/drugs, sex, fighting and the very act of rocking itself. This also applies if your dad's Proper Music of choice is rap/hip-hop, but the fourth topic will be the very act of rapping itself instead.

A great band to use to study the rock-based variety of these topics is AC/DC. If you don't know who they are – and given the fact as an entity they're older than email, Chicken McNuggets and VHS (a way of watching films that was replaced by DVD that was replaced by Blu-ray that was replaced by streaming so you'll never actually own anything ever again), you probably don't know who they are – ask your dad about them.

Be warned, he may well shout 'ACKER DACKER' at you and strut across the room playing air guitar like a giraffe with leg cramps. All this is perfectly normal and is no cause for alarm.

Covering all of drink/sex/fighting/rocking, AC/DC have songs called 'Have a Drink on Me', 'Sink the Pink' (subtlety is not part of their charm), 'Spoilin' for a Fight' (see?) and 'Let There Be Rock' respectively. Proper Music can cover more than one topic in the same song, but these guys view this approach as needlessly fiddly. When dads talk about Proper Music, AC/DC are as good an example as any.

Dads will often own physical reminders of how they used to listen to Proper Music all the time, such as a range of T-shirts featuring band names that sound like the punchlines to terrible jokes (Limp Bizkit, Puddle Of Mudd and The The were all serious adults that released actual albums that people bought with their own money and everything – no, really). He will occasionally try wearing one of these until he realises his body shape has transformed over the last few decades from slender caterpillar – and not to a moth, but to a fatter caterpillar.

Your dad may also have a shelving unit full of vinyl records that he will tell you sound far better than the audio quality you get from a computer, despite the fact they're basically large plastic coasters that have had stuff gouged into them. You may never get to disprove your dad's theory, because it's quite likely that he has hundreds of records but doesn't actually have a record player to play them on. This is no reason to get rid of them however, he will tetchily insist.

Worst of all is if your dad owns a musical instrument – most typically a guitar like AC/DC play when they're singing about the fact they have Big Balls (like I said, they are *not* a subtle group). Touching his guitar is a crime comparable to running around the house blindfold waving a blowtorch about. He has the tuning just the way he wants it. It rests on an expensive stand for a reason. It. Is. Not. A. Toy.

No, it's a limited-edition Firestar CherryPhoenix with the triple-coil low-strung pickdowns and the flat-wedge tuning stock, just like Pete Alfalfa played on Cheese Repellent's seminal debut album *Emetic Sunrise*. (All of the above is entirely fictional, but is indistinguishable from when your dad starts talking about his guitar – or, if you're very unlucky, what he will refer to as his 'axe'. Throw in a few made-up phrases yourself to see if he notices or if he tries to style it out: 'Dad, does your guitar have the 1986 dolphin-body shape, or is it a Kansas remodel with the Cardi B interior?')

What Dad Says: 'I used to be in a band myself, we gigged loads back in the day.'

What Dad Means: 'I spent three months in my dad's mate's garage playing rhythm guitar, trying to learn any of the three chords to 'Teenage Kicks' before we had a massive row over what the band logo was going to look like and we split up.'

If your dad owns a musical instrument, he is absolutely convinced that he could have been a successful musician and there is an alternate universe out there where he's currently giving a press conference ahead of his latest worldwide tour, in which he denies the rumours that he and Margot Robbie are dating while he grins from ear to ear. If you ever have a conversation with your dad about his musician days (and there are few things on earth he would like to happen more) and you see his eyes glaze over slightly, this is where he is.

A dispute over a band logo is just one of the Sliding

Doors moments that could have shifted him away from becoming an area manager for a freight shipping company and becoming a Rock God Colossus instead. The margins of fate are microscopically slim, and all it takes is for something as tiny as having no lucky breaks, no contacts in the music industry, being in the wrong place at the wrong time, having no charisma or songwriting ability or sex appeal, or having to say 'Hang on a second, I know this next bit' before trying a tricky guitar solo containing more than seven notes.

What Dad Says: 'I'm off to see Cheap Falafel on their reunion tour tonight. Don't wait up, who knows when I'll be home!'

What Dad Means: 'I'm not staying past the first encore, I've got a 9 a.m. meeting.'

Dads like to go to music gigs. It gets them out of the house, and there are times when they will earnestly tell the family that they are all out of rawl plugs and urgently need to drive to a B&Q fifteen miles away, just to give them an excuse. So for your dad, the prospect of two recovering alcoholics, the son of the original drummer filling in for dad (RIP), and a singer on his third marriage and fourth facelift playing an album from two decades ago is an exciting one.

Your dad will rarely go to a music gig to see a new band, or even a band that has troubled the charts since you were born. He's had a long week, tickets are expensive these days, and the last thing he wants to hear are the dreaded words 'Here's one from our new album' – which signals the opportunity for him to go to the toilet for his sixth pee of the evening.

There are bands out there, no doubt, who play the kind of Proper Music he likes. Okay, these bands are in their early twenties and in the music press they refer to the sound of their music – which was also popular when your dad arranged his first overdraft – as 'retro', but he would probably enjoy them if he gave them a try.

But it's much safer to listen to the back catalogue of Cheap Falafel in the week leading up to the gig. Like putting on a pair of old slippers (Old Slippers is another favourite band of your dad's who will be getting back together in a few months' time, coincidentally).

There's the song that was playing when he first danced with your mum. The album he had on in the background when he studied at university (a fifty-minute-long album, so it covered the amount of daily studying time with room to spare). The double album where they experimented with that jazz trio. He really hopes they don't play anything off that one at the gig.

On the day of the gig itself, your dad will have his

dinner early so he can set off in plenty of time to see Cheap Falafel. When he was young this would be so he could line his stomach with food ahead of the dozen pints served in plastic glasses he was about to consume, and so he could be there when the doors opened to run to the barriers at the front, close enough to the band to be able to estimate in weeks how long it had been since any of them had changed their socks.

Nowadays, he wants a decent meal inside of him because he's damned if he's going to pay fifteen quid inside the venue for a hot dog that looks like it died from anaemia and has lain stricken under a heat lamp for so long it's at the midway point between hot dog and pork jerky. And he wants to set off early to find free residential parking within walking distance of the venue, rather than paying more per hour for venue parking than he earned in his first job.

What Dad Says: 'The best place to stand is by the mixing desk, the sound there is amazing.'

What Dad Means: 'I wouldn't go near the mosh pit these days if you threw my wallet, car keys and youngest grandchild into it.'

Getting to the venue early means your dad can position himself against the mixing desk and try to start an awkward conversation with the sound engineer by throwing in some vaguely technical musical terms ('How is the low-end EQ in this room? Do you find you have to baffle the midrange much?'), which the engineer will ignore because this is their job, tonight is just another band to them, and if Jesus himself turned up to do an acoustic set the only comment the sound engineer would make is if the Son of God was a bit of a diva during the soundcheck.

The mixing desk is usually situated near to the bar, giving your dad plenty of opportunities to wave a tenner around at the overwhelmed bar staff while pondering under his breath if he is actually invisible when the younger, more attractive gig-goers get served first. As a bonus, he gets to incredulously ask the server if they're absolutely sure that's how much a pint of flat Diet Coke is meant to cost, forgetting the fact that the guy with the neck tattoo behind the bar is unlikely to be the owner of the venue, and probably has little input into pricing policy. He *does* have a say on who he and his colleagues choose to ignore, though, as your dad will learn as the evening progresses.

Stood near the back of the venue, when Cheap Falafel shamble on stage, your dad will be unable to see how much they have aged, which is a good thing because in the back of his mind he's vaguely aware that they're all pretty much the same age as him. Stage lighting and failing eyesight will mean Cheap Falafel are also unable to see how old their audience are getting or the fact the room is half-full.

What people *will* be able to see, regrettably, is the dancing. More specifically, your dad dancing. A responsible publisher will have ensured this book is plastered with warnings that this was going to come up and which pages to avoid if you'd rather not think about it, but if you're still reading, here we are and we may as well get on with it.

Your dad will be dancing.

The term 'dancing' is, unlike your dad, very flexible and can encompass a wide range of movement (again, unlike your dad). It's unlikely that the director of the Royal National Ballet will be nearby, nudge their friend and say, 'Okay, we've got our Romeo sorted for next month' at the sight of your dad slowly grooving away to Cheap Falafel.

The typical dad dance will involve a low level of physical activity that ensures his drink never leaves his hand and he runs zero risk of spilling a drop of Diet Coke. The ballet director is more likely to suspect that your dad is trying to surreptitiously dislodge his underwear than that dancing is occurring.

Wobbly plastic glass in hand, the eyes may half-close in a show of Getting Into It. The degree of Getting Into It is further signified by the head nodding slightly along with the beat. This means the dancing, if dancing is what it must be called, is sometimes interrupted when two unsighted dads collide into each other and their reverie is broken.

With his free hand, your dad may try a physical expression of his feelings towards Cheap Falafel. Finger-wagging in a non-censorious manner. A flat hand waved up and down like it's stuck out of the window of a speeding car, perhaps. Or a closed fist shaking an invisible maraca. Just be thankful he didn't bring along an actual maraca.

Aware that he may look like one of those cheap plastic sunflowers that move when you play music, your dad will also drag his feet into the proceedings – and with a level of coordination that makes it look like they were dragged in against their will. Again, nothing too strenuous will be attempted. It will look like he's stepping out of a pair of old slippers (which reminds him that he really must book those Old Slippers tickets) or treading enough grapes to make half a bottle of wine.

The only variation on the above is when Cheap Falafel play one of their three hits, when your dad's free hand will be held above his head and start pointing at the band, properly identifying them as the band who released this song and are currently playing it. He will shout/sing about 47 per cent of the actual lyrics at a volume that the sound engineer behind him will mercifully ensure is inaudible.

When the gig is over, or at least when Cheap Falafel have played all of the songs your dad can remember, he will briefly peruse the merchandise table out in the lobby and pretend that he is weighing up whether he wants to buy a purple vinyl version of their jazz experimental double album *Nepal McCartney* or a T-shirt. The T-shirt is not a viable option, however, as most of their audience look like your dad, and by now they will only have it in small, medium and large. And your dad passed the point of 'large' T-shirts fitting him a long time ago.

On the drive home, your dad will listen to the same Cheap Falafel songs he's just heard, admitting to himself – but nobody else when they ask him how the gig was – that he prefers the recorded versions over the live versions, which were slower, went on for far too long, and did they really need to be so *loud*?

This serves as a distraction from his bladder, which is full of overpriced Diet Coke. He regrets not going for a final pee before leaving, then remembers what the toilets looked like and stops regretting his decision. John Lennon once sang that happiness is a warm gun, but your dad would counter that, right now, it's a clean toilet.

The Golf Trip

What Dad Says: 'I only do it for the exercise.'

What Dad Means: 'I really wish you could
   drive the cart straight into the bar.'

Typical Dad Joke: 'I bought four pairs of
   golf trousers but I got a hole in one.'

Your dad is an avid sports fan. Golf, tennis, football, running, rugby – there isn't a physical activity he doesn't enjoy sitting on the sofa watching while criticising the performance on display.

'They keep cutting back in on the inside when there's space down the flanks to exploit with a transitional pass in the final third,' he will loftily announce, thinking you have forgotten the time he had to wear a shoulder brace for a fortnight after struggling to escape from a rollneck sweater that no longer fitted him.

That footballer may have trained since the age of four. He may earn a six-figure weekly salary. He may have the resting heart rate of a boulder. He may well

be the pinnacle of concentration, physique and dedication. But your dad has watched every episode of
Match of the Day since 1987 (even that one when Gary
Lineker went on strike), so who's to say who knows
better?

You sometimes suspect that his dedication to sport
may have more to do with a dedication to not having
to help around the house with other things. It is of
course entirely possible that he always had an abiding
interest in second-division Norwegian handball, but
it is also possible that he isn't a huge fan of emptying
the dishwasher.

A good way of telling how invested he is in the sport
he claims to be watching is by measuring his levels of
tetchiness. Interruptions, for instance. Walk in front
of the screen during a vital moment, ask him whether
he knows where the barbecue tongs are kept (this is
especially effective when asked in January, there's a
foot of snow outside and he knows full well you've no
intention of cremating some sausages in minus-three
degrees), or start setting up a series link recording on
the satellite box for a documentary series about canoes.

Keep track of when your dad gets annoyed and
shouts at the screen. If he's put on some bobsleigh-
ing (outside of the Olympics, of course – during the
Olympics it is entirely acceptable to become irration-
ally invested in minor sports you go on to ignore for

the following forty-seven months until the next Olympics, despite your earnestly vocalised intention to start watching your local curling team when the Games are finished) and is just randomly shouting at the Germans for shaving 7/100ths of a second off the Finnish split time, it's probable he's just watching it to lie low.

Genuine tetchiness is impossible to mistake but is very easy to exacerbate when it happens. Telling him that there's always next year for his team to try to win (even when – in fact *especially* when – it's a competition like the World Cup that isn't played annually) has never in the history of sports-watching been known to calm a dad down. Neither has pointing out that a player keeps making the same mistake that lets the opposition score, or asking whether they meant to do that very clumsy thing that they quite obviously didn't mean to do.

That's not to say that sport doesn't bring joy into your dad's life – it often does. Who can forget the time he danced a conga line out of the living room and into the street with his mates, waving his replica shirt around his head and spraying beer into the air, when his team won the league? Not the old woman with a heart condition who lives across the road from you, certainly.

And you can clearly remember every wicket England took during a particular Ashes tour in Australia, although you would have preferred a good night's sleep before school in the morning rather than waking up every half hour to 'HOWZAT?' from downstairs.

He used to play a bit, back in the day. What he used to 'play a bit' entirely depends on the sport you're watching at the time and how plausible it is that he competed in it even as a schoolboy. If you sprouted past him during a growth spurt by the age of eleven and now have a commanding view of his bald spot glinting away from a foot below, he will struggle to convince you that a potential career in basketball was ever an option.

Something like cricket or football has a level of plausible deniability to it, and he can explain why he never hit the big time without having to resort to saying, 'Because I was terrible at it and had all the physical coordination of a newborn calf wearing skates trying to run down an up escalator.' It's possible he was concentrating on his studies (a good way to segue into telling you to pull your socks up at school), or he met your mother and wanted to spend all his time with her rather than falling out of a nightclub in his twenties entwined in the arms of a pop singer. And an old sporting injury that curtailed his career can get him out of all manner of things, especially given that it has the magical ability to move to whichever part of his body might be needed.

However, the only sport he still competitively takes part in nowadays is golf – as long as you have a very flexible definition of the words 'competitively' and 'sport'.

What Dad Says: 'My handicap is
really coming down this year.'

What Dad Means: 'It's months since I managed
to shank the ball into the car park.'

Your dad takes his golf seriously. This is evidenced by how much he sulks when he has to cancel playing a round because of trifling prior commitments such as a family funeral or because the weather stupidly refuses to remain a dry, windless seventy degrees on the rock just off the north Atlantic where he lives.

And nobody would willingly dress like your dad does for golf unless they absolutely loved what they were doing. The golf shoes are an unavoidable item of apparel (or 'piece of kit', as he will insist on calling every golf-related bit of equipment he owns, from his clubs right down to the ball-washer you're not allowed to giggle at whenever he mentions it; other terms you're not allowed to giggle at include 'wood', 'grip', 'shaft' and the brand 'Titleist') if he wants to be allowed on the course. But the rest of his golfing ensemble makes you wish he'd leave for the course under a blanket like a defendant leaving court after being found guilty of doing something awful to a swan.

Slacks. There's no other word for them. He can call them 'comfort action-wear' as much as he likes, but your dad goes to play golf wearing slacks. And nobody cares if the catalogue says they're 'Cobalt Aqua'. Dad, we all know they're powder blue. This is topped off with a polo-neck sweater that makes him look like he works for a fast-food chain that only employs people who live in nursing homes.

This is if you're lucky and the weather is warm. On colder days (and your dad will insist that a round of golf is still possible even when the news is showing footage of trees strewn across motorways and market towns under five feet of water), he will be wearing a jumper that he presumably found in the bins behind a charity shop.

This is how everybody dresses at the course, you will be told. You have to take his word for it, because he would rather throw his clubs into a woodchipper than have his golf world and his rest-of-my-life world collide, taking away his one safe sanctuary.

Speaking of his clubs, they are a mystery all of their own. He needs every one of them, apparently, despite the fact 80 per cent of them look identical, except for the heads that increase in degrees of thickness so small that surgical instruments are probably engineered with less precision. Having seen your dad manoeuvre a rake out of the shed, destroying several plant pots and a hibernating hedgehog in the process, it seems unlikely that he is able to wield a golf club with enough finesse to notice if it has a cigarette paper's worth of additional metal on it.

Of course, this doesn't stop him from dreamily browsing websites and magazines that advertise even more clubs for him to buy, with the promise that the latest in carbon graphite tungsten weight-shift modulators will make all the difference to his game while he hacks away at the ball like a mob boss in an abandoned warehouse settling a dispute with a rival's skull. The only difference between him and world champion golfer Fuzzy McIntyre is the fact Fuzzy owns a £700 driver and he doesn't (you may find this hard to believe, but while I did make up the name of that golfer, I didn't make up how much a single golf club can cost).

Whenever the subject of how much he paid for his golf clubs comes up, there is a shifty, uncomfortable silence from your dad, like your mum just found an unexplained florist bill on his credit card statement. He might tell you he locks his clubs away to keep them safe from burglars – that section of the criminal fraternity who famously break into houses wearing salmon-pink sweaters draped over their shoulders. But it's more likely that he doesn't want you googling how much a set of clubs like his cost and start asking questions like why the family has to make do with an incontinent fridge-freezer that's older than you are when he has a small fortune locked in his bedroom wardrobe, each with their own little knitted hat.

What Dad Says: 'Tee-off is at eleven but it's usually busy today, so I'll be back late.'

What Dad Means: 'We're all terrible at this, it could take all day.'

Your dad has a set of friends he always plays golf with, safe in the knowledge that only the four of them know how awful they all are at the game – and assured that whatever handicaps they report to their respective families when they get back home will never be challenged.

The only exceptions to this are the rare occasions when your dad is invited to play golf in a work capacity, sending a chill down his spine in anticipation of his incompetence being found out and his boss asking him whether this is his first time holding a putter. Your dad has weighed up the relative merits of getting on in his job by going to more work-related golf events and having complete strangers mutter 'Jesus, mind the windows' during his backswing, and has decided that maybe his career isn't everything.

Your dad's golf friends can be summarised as follows . . .

The Organiser: This is the one who makes sure the course has been booked for the right day and time, and that everyone has coughed up the green fees. He keeps score during the round and is happy to drive to and from the course so everyone else can get as refreshed as possible once they've finished. The Organiser knows that the group probably wouldn't socialise with him if he didn't provide these services and has made peace with that.

He's also a far better golfer than anyone else in the group, and knows that whenever they joke about him 'taking it too seriously' they are inwardly a boiling, seething mass of resentment who would love to smack a 300-yard drive right next to the pin so they can rub it in his face.

All The Gear: This is the one who makes your dad's set of clubs look like they were cobbled together in his backyard out of tree branches and pebbles. All The Gear's annual expenditure on golf equipment could sustain an entire village in one of the countries where the sweatshops make his gloves.

All The Gear has his own indoor driving range simulator at home, with a photometric radar assessing his swing that could be used on an aircraft carrier to monitor enemy planes. All The Gear has a guy he goes to who patiently whittles, moulds, lengthens and calibrates his clubs to perfectly complement his game.

All The Gear has a handicap of 47.

It's Not Even Noon: INEN views golf as the pleasant, relaxing, leafy backdrop to his descent into intoxication. If he simply sat in a Wetherspoons pub from eleven in the morning until early evening, working his way through so much Jack Daniel's that the staff got a new bottle for the optics the second he walked through the door, that would be a bit tragic. But if he's wearing shoes with little tassels on them while somebody else drives him around in a buggy (he is no longer allowed to drive the golf cart since The Incident), this is a healthy pastime that just so happens to involve booze.

INEN has the heaviest golf bag of the group, which initially made All The Gear worry that he'd invested in some piece of kit (thanks, Dad) that he hadn't heard of yet. Further inspection showed that the bottom of his golf bag was cold, due to the cans of Staropramen he'd stashed in there, and the mystery was solved.

During holes 1–6, INEN is pleasant company, cracking jokes with the rest of the group while sipping from a hip flask that has 'Glenfiddich' engraved on it. He bought this in the mistaken belief that it was a golf course. Holes 7–12 see him become gradually quieter, as for him the challenge of hitting the golf ball is mostly about squinting until the number of golf balls he can see is down to one. By about the 16th hole he is dozing contentedly in the golf buggy, occasionally snoring himself awake and saying 'Good shot' regardless of whether anyone even has a club in their hand.

What Dad Says: 'Did you miss me?'

What Dad Means: 'I missed you.'

Your dad couldn't live without golf in his life as a pressure-release valve from stress. He genuinely loves it when he manages to hit the ball sweetly and to be out amongst the gently undulating greens. He treasures the moments of silence on the course when The Organiser isn't reminding everyone about the renewal of their annual membership fees, All The Gear's laser range finder isn't beeping away at him, and It's Not Even Noon isn't singing Pogues songs while peeing in a bush.

But if he's being completely honest, after a few hours in the company of the people he plays golf with, he'd much rather be next to you on the sofa criticising Tiger Woods's putting. Actually, he could really do with a putter like that . . .

Christmas

What Dad Says: 'We only make a
   fuss for the kids, really.'

What Dad Means: 'If the house isn't stuffed like
   a medieval banquet full of food I will cry.'

Typical Dad Joke: (Shakes a very small gift)
   'Is it a mountain bike?'

The old Andy Williams song says that Christmas is the most wonderful time of the year, and your dad would wholeheartedly agree, although Williams cites as evidence for this the fact that there'll be 'kids jingle belling', a situation your dad finds less than ideal. Any toddler that insists on repeated jingle belling within earshot of your dad will soon find the offending item confiscated and relocated to a high shelf until further notice.

   The build-up to Christmas starts sometime in November, once Halloween has been safely dealt with by your dad purchasing a shopping trolley full of sweets, dimming all the lights on 31 October so no trick-or-treaters know he's at home, then steadily making his way through the bucket of fun-sized chocolate bars as 'they'll only go off otherwise'.

You have learned that pointing out they have a best before date that will see them through to next Halloween is a futile venture that will be met with a small Bounty bar being launched in your direction by way of a response (he won't eat those ones because the coconut gets stuck in his teeth).

The first step is to drag the Christmas decorations out of the loft. This is a joyful few hours in the household, marked by bitter recriminations, muffled profanities and the ongoing possibility of seeing his feet crashing through a bedroom ceiling.

During his time in the loft he will snag several holes in one of the few shirts he owns that is relatively stain-free, despite your mum telling him to put his decorating clothes on beforehand. Your dad will then inevitably stumble across an unmarked cardboard box full of stuff he promised he was going to throw away years ago, which will spark a prolonged case for the defence using the words 'collectible', 'heritage' and 'cherished memories' to justify hanging on to a load of Plymouth Argyle football programmes from the mid-1990s ('This one has an interview with Nigel Martyn in it – he played for Leeds, you know. He was the first million-pound goal— OKAY, FINE, I'LL THROW THEM OUT LATER.')

Once the decorations have been located, a decision has to be made on whether to buy a real tree this year or persist with the plastic tree whose age can be determined by the fact it has Woolworths branding on the box.

Your dad will argue that it would be fun to go out and pick a real tree (it won't) and the whole family can make an afternoon of it (they won't) and you can get sprays nowadays that stop the needles from shedding (they don't) and he will make sure the carpet stays clean (he won't) and it will make the whole house smell festive (it won't).

Your dad will then bring down the fake tree from the loft. The topic of real Christmas trees will be packed away in the loft of his mind until this time next year.

This is the perfect time to put on your shoes, grab your coat and sprint towards the door, inventing any excuse possible for needing to leave the house for an hour or so. Tell everyone you need to go and buy a jar of preserved lemons from a local delicatessen. Tell them you've started volunteering for an hour every weekend at a nearby vole sanctuary. Anything, it doesn't matter, but think of something to get out of the house before you become entangled – literally and figuratively – in the Unravelling of the Lights.

What Dad Says: 'These lights are looking a
   bit tired, maybe we buy a new set?'

What Dad Means: 'I would rather French-kiss
   a food blender than untie another knot.'

Coil them in small sections with a rubber band. Wrap them around a coat hanger from one side to the other. Squeeze them into a ball rather than loops. Rub cooking oil on them and dance naked by the light of a full moon while reciting the whole of 'In-A-Gadda-Da-Vida' backwards while you stuff them into a cursed shoebox.

Everyone has a tip on how to store Christmas-tree lights, and none of them work.

Historians will tell you that Christmas lights were invented by a Phrygian named Gordias, and he used them to attach his cart to an ox when he ran out of hemp. The Gordian knot of tree lights perplexed the eminent philosophers of the day, until Alexander the Great arrived many years later and uttered his most famous quote, 'Oh sod this, I can't be bothered,' before hacking at them with his sword.

Physicists will argue that they prove the existence of

quantum realms, with the lights occupying superpositions in forty-seven different realities simultaneously, meaning that every knot you untie opens up the possibility of billions of knots further along. This is the basis of string theory in astrophysics, with some scientists believing that the Big Bang event was caused by a creature of unimaginable size and power losing their rag and throwing away an infinite set of lights, which became every star in the observable universe. The origins of the universe may therefore be inferred by following the stars backwards until a telescope powerful enough can be built to find the astral plug socket.

Astrophysicists are an odd bunch.

Back on Earth, your dad will start the tree-light untangling in a good mood. He may even chuckle about how long this always takes and pour himself a small glass of eggnog, Baileys or other sickly booze that nobody touches outside of Christmas while he works on them. Slowly but surely the hummed Christmas carols will cease and be replaced with sighs of greater volume and significance. Furniture will be pushed to one side so the string can be laid out in full and the knots more easily identified. If you failed to flee in time, you will be asked to take one end of the lights and slowly walk backwards so the level of multidimensional entanglement can be better assessed.

After an operation more complicated, fraught and delicate than defusing a bomb while sat in a tumble dryer, the lights will eventually be one straight line from plug to tip. Only then can they be plugged in to find that they don't light up and one of the bulbs is faulty.

Next Christmas, you will be quicker on your feet.

What Dad Says: 'Anyone want a snack?'

What Dad Means: 'I'm going to the
kitchen. I may be some time.'

The run-up to Christmas is an ongoing battle between your mum and your dad over what constitutes 'Christmas food' and how far away from 25 December Christmas food can be eaten. As far as your mum is concerned, anything containing cheese, sugar, nutmeg, bacon, pastry or pickle is strictly off-limits until Christmas Eve. A mental switch is flicked on in her head at this point, and you will suddenly be offered food every twelve minutes during waking hours well into January, because it all needs 'using up'.

This is a fancy gastronomic term whereby the chef prepares their meal based on how likely the ingredients are to grow mould in the next day or so and therefore need 'using up'. A ciabatta sandwich filled with Wensleydale and cranberry, pigs in blankets and battered prawns makes much more sense in this context.

Your dad takes a more relaxed view of Christmas food, reasoning that if the pantry finds itself out of cheese footballs, honey-roasted cashew nuts, Twiglets, mini pork pies, satsumas (for the vitamins – it's important to try to keep a healthy diet even at Christmas) or After Eight mints, he can always buy more.

And it will, and he will.

Ordinarily, food is something that happens at discrete times of the day. So much so, the English language even invented words like 'breakfast' and 'dinner' to describe when it happens. Christmas sees the blurring of these boundaries, and your dad's hands with their opposable thumbs stop being beautiful examples of evolution that have allowed humanity to manipulate their environment, wield fire, create art and explore outer space, and start being tools to make sure his mouth remains full of dry-roasted peanuts.

This can lead to a form of choice paralysis that will make your dad do the unthinkable: leave the fridge door open for minutes at a time while he decides what to eat next. The cold inside the fridge is usually regarded as a resource more precious than platinum, and he would no more leave the door open than a pilot would in a 747 when halfway across the Atlantic. But faced with so many options – does piccalilli go with cauliflower-cheese leftovers? Can I just stick a spoon in that pot of brandy cream and eat it like a yoghurt? – he enters into a kind of prediabetic trance that can only be broken by reminding him he hasn't opened the bag of mixed nuts yet.

What Dad Says: 'It's about spending time with your family.'

What Dad Means: 'It's about the presents but I'm not allowed to say that.'

Every family has their own routine for Christmas Day itself, and every single routine except the one your own family follows is downright weird.

For instance, some people allow their kids to open one present on Christmas Eve, a kind of teaser trailer for the main event the following day. Your dad views this kind of lax attitude towards gift-opening as morally bankrupt, and assumes that engaging in such hedonistic self-indulgence is the kind of thing that resulted in Russian peasants in 1918 deciding that the Tsar and his family had one too many Fabergé eggs and one too few holes in their foreheads.

The Christmas Day routine hinges on three things, none of which your dad feels is up for discussion:

1. When and how the presents are opened
2. When Christmas dinner is eaten
3. Whether you watch the King's speech

Other factors come into play, such as dragging everyone out for a bracing Christmas Day walk so you can meet other grim-faced families walking in the opposite direction wishing they were back home pouring hot chocolate into themselves in front of a Pixar movie, and whether your dad should 'get out from underneath everyone's feet' while dinner is being prepared by popping down to the pub. But these are the three key events.

The third is the simplest to address – it is based on a yes/no answer, and depends on how traditional your dad is, how old any visiting relatives are, and whether your dad can stay awake long enough into the day to find out how the Commonwealth is getting on and whether the monarch is concerned about those living on their own at this difficult time of year (not concerned enough to invite any of them round for dinner, of course).

Your dad will be very vocal about when Christmas dinner is eaten, despite having little to no direct input into cooking it other than insisting he carve the turkey to ensure he gets the best leg, and trying in vain to set fire to the brandy on top of the Christmas pudding that nobody really likes anyway and that will be one of the hardest sells when your mum starts 'using up' food in earnest.

Breakfast will have been fancy in some way because it seems irreligious to celebrate the birth of Jesus with a bowl of Coco Pops, so your dad will have enjoyed a smoked salmon and cream cheese bagel washed down with a Bucks Fizz, because orange juice magically stops it from looking like what it is – drinking wine before 9 a.m.

But that leaves hours of grazing until the 'right' time for the big event. Anything earlier than midday is madness, clearly, and anything later than 6 p.m. is a form of prolonged torture for a dad's stomach that has been trained to expand for weeks by the careful and constant addition of crisps. Waiting until the BBC show their exclusive film premiere that has been available on streaming for six months is the kind of slow agony that would have the head of the Spanish Inquisition asking the lads to tone it down a bit.

Whenever the 'right' time is, the dinner itself has several component parts.

The preparation: Realising you don't have enough plates/cutlery for visiting relatives, meaning younger family members like yourself end up eating a roast dinner out of a cereal bowl using a measuring spoon. Timing it so all the elements are brown/hot/not going to give anyone food poisoning simultaneously. Finding a forgotten foodstuff in the fridge and hurriedly microwaving it. Doling the gravy out evenly onto each plate, in the sure and certain knowledge there will always be 20 per cent less of it than the ideal amount. All while your dad asks from the living room whether anyone needs a hand and praying they don't say yes.

The consumption: Before anyone has a single mouthful, sufficient praise has to be given for how great the Christmas dinner looks, with special attention given to the crispiness of the roast potatoes. There is no praise higher – no Nobel Prize given, no bronze statue erected, no library named in your honour – than telling somebody who cooked you a Christmas dinner that their roast potatoes are really crispy.

A silence then falls over the room as everybody attacks their food like some angry Bolshevik is going to whip their plate away without warning. Your dad will make appreciative moans like somebody is giving him a foot massage under the table, occasionally pointing at a pig in a blanket or a honeyed parsnip with his fork and nodding. When they talk about peace on earth and goodwill to all men, this is the stuff they have in mind.

Further compliments are then made by your dad when he loudly announces he couldn't possibly eat another mouthful, they'll have to roll him to bed later, his eyes were bigger than his belly and so on. This is signified ceremonially by pushing his plate away, cutlery placed on top, and gesturing that he's done, like a boxing referee declaring a knockout.

The aftermath: For the rest of the day, your dad will reappear from a visit to the kitchen with the half-eaten remains of a potato, a sliver of turkey or a gobbet of cauliflower cheese. Dipped in bread sauce if he's feeling adventurous. As good as the meal itself tasted, the component parts nabbed afterwards from the roasting trays piled high in the kitchen always taste better.

What Dad Says: 'That's not your main present.'

What Dad Means: 'I'll wait to see which one you really like and that will be your main present.'

The main question, as the family rue their decision not to wear trousers with elasticated waistbands, is whether the Christmas presents have already been opened or not. There is no greater shock in life than the first Christmas you spend with another family – usually that of a girlfriend or boyfriend – and seeing how they open their presents compares to how your dad always said it should be done. There are some real lunatics out there.

If he gave into his baser desires, your dad would wait until everybody was awake and dressed and had their first coffee/tea/third glass of Bucks Fizz (because the bottle has been opened now so it'll only go flat, actually). There would be piles of gifts placed around the living room with the recipients' names above them on Post-it notes. He would produce a referee's whistle, blow it sharply, and everyone would lunge at their gifts like a set of extras from *The Walking Dead*, tearing at the wrapping paper as if it were an enticing-looking bit of leg.

Dad knows about deferred gratification. He read an article about it – or at least he skipped to the end to read the conclusion. He's heard about those families – strange, ascetic families with wills of iron, pure souls and all the joie de vivre of a dilapidated church – who open their gifts slowly throughout the whole day (rather than in a flurry of arms and Sellotape in a twenty-minute frenzy at 10 a.m., before wading knee-deep through wrapping paper to go and get another Bucks Fizz). One by one, over twelve agonising hours, presents are selected from the single pile while the rest of the family look on, smiling beatifically. The recipient will read the label, thank the person who gave it, and slowly unpeel the wrapping paper so carefully it could be ironed and sold in a card shop without anybody noticing. They will comment at length about what a thoughtful gift it is, thanking the gift-giver once more, then the rest of the long day carries on until at some point in the future the next gift is opened. Hour after hour after hour like that.

Perverts, basically.

That is not the Christmas your dad knows and loves, but he knows that if everyone did open their presents too quickly, he'd regret it deep down. What your dad is looking for is somewhere in the middle. He's far too impatient to see what that bottle-shaped gift for him is to wait until the time of night they start swearing on the TV to open it, but on the other hand, he enjoys seeing everyone's faces as they open their gifts. Especially when he wraps an old iPhone box and puts a bag of Maltesers in it just to see your reaction.

He misses the days when you thought Father Christmas provided the gifts, stumbling noisily into your bedroom on Christmas Eve smelling like mince pies and lager to place a pillowcase ('Santa is not forking out a fiver for a gift sack when we – he – has perfectly good bedding at home') at the foot of your bed.

Those days are gone, but what he can still enjoy is the experience of seeing you hold up a gift hopefully, open it excitedly, confirm it was that thing you really,

really wanted, give him a hug of thanks and tell him how happy it's made you.

Nothing brings him greater happiness than telling you you'd better like it because it cost a bloody fortune and he's not made of money. Joy to the world!

The Holiday

What Dad Says: 'It's a chance to
    experience a different culture.'

What Dad Means: 'It's a whole new
    world of crisp flavours.'

Typical Dad Joke: 'Do they do egg
    and chips here?' – he is only *mostly*
    joking when he says this.

Family holidays are a way for you all to spend more time together, relax in comfortable surroundings and really bond with each other. In much the same way that being fired out of a cannon is a way to experience life at different velocities and altitudes while gaining valuable life lessons in what landing in a crumpled heap feels like.

When you were very young, the actual destination of your holidays mattered a lot less. Being slathered in factor 347 suncream next to a swimming pool primarily filled with a mixture of sweat, urine and factor 347 suncream feels much the same to a baby whether that pool is in Majorca, Fiji or Rhyl.

As a toddler, your dad didn't feel the need to culturally enrich you when you were on holiday by pushing a pram around a set of ruins that might be an ancient temple dedicated to the god of lettuce or an administration building where they collected taxes from farmers growing some vegetable nobody eats anymore. There's no way he'd be paying another ten quid to hire the poorly translated audio guide to explain what he was looking at in any case ('Many in the ancient of periods, mass people are travelling to this location with the gourds for trading, as can be seen in the stones above you to your behind'), so your understanding of what you were looking at would be much the same as his.

Equally, a visit to a genuine, authentic village where genuine, authentic villagers go about their genuine, authentic business as they have genuinely, authentically done for hundreds of years would be lost on the pair of you when you were that age. You would be too young to even notice that the genuine, authentic villagers would much rather be back in their houses watching Sky Sports while sat on their sofas than trying to sell your dad a hand-woven bracelet for the same price as the entire outfit he was wearing.

In those days, when searching for a holiday

location, your dad would use an algebraic equation with 'price of beer', 'price of flights/accommodation' and 'average temperature' as the variables. He's tried to explain the equation to you but you don't understand it, because this is the sort of thing schools try to teach you in the last few weeks before the summer holidays when 93 per cent of your brain is already sat on a beach.

But in later years, your dad would come to feel that a holiday should at least try to have some sort of educational component, to justify the fact it cost three times as much as it would have cost if he was allowed to yank you out of school for the last week of term when you weren't learning any algebra.

A castle or Roman fort is always a safe bet to meet the educational requirement. They usually have old swords or paintings of people having arrows fired at them, which is always entertaining. You can usually get round them in about an hour without feeling you've skipped anything, or succumbing to Museum Legs (a condition afflicting the lower limbs of people who have gone into an art gallery or museum or whatnot with the best of cultural intentions, but have gradually become so bored the sensation pools in the lower limbs as a dull ache that can only be alleviated by leaving the establishment in question). And they're usually within walking distance of really good pubs that have wonky floors, regional draught ales, and the kind of hearty homecooked meals on offer that your dad will fondly reminisce about months later.

If you're going abroad, anything that doesn't exist on your local high street can technically count as experiencing a foreign culture and therefore be called educational. That said, even a visit to the McDonald's in Spain can count as doing something new, so long as you order the McIberica, a burger with Iberico ham and Manchego cheese on it that is a thing that actually exists.

What Dad Says: 'I'll get some supplies for the apartment.'

What Dad Means: 'I'm off to the supermarket to buy weird stuff.'

In order to keep the costs of the holiday down, on the day you arrive your dad will buy food and drink from the nearby store in the resort, in order to prepare meals for the family so you don't need to eat at a restaurant all the time. On the face of it this seems like a sensible idea and a chance for more family bonding, as everyone will be mucking in to help prepare a fresh, delicious meal made from local produce that can be enjoyed on the balcony in the sunshine.

However.

Your dad cannot be trusted to do this shopping trip on his own. The zeal with which he volunteers to go food shopping, and the fact he actually suggests it without prompting, should be your first clue that this can and will end up going very badly wrong. If your family makes the mistake of letting your dad go on this shopping run unaccompanied, draw up a list of what you would come back with if you were doing the shopping. It almost certainly includes some or all of the following:

Bottled water
Bread
Cheese/ham
Tomatoes
Eggs
Orange juice
Tea/coffee
Milk

None of these items will be in the shopping bags your dad is carrying when he gets back to the holiday apartment. Those bags will contain some or all of the following:

A type of Fanta you can't get in the UK
A jar of olives with a name that sounds a bit rude
Six varieties of crisps with flavours like
     cinnamon, fried egg and Nutella

Milka and/or Toblerone chocolate that has
   already melted in the packet
Two bags of ice (your apartment does not have
   a freezer)
Sixteen bottles of local beer (your apartment
   does not have a bottle opener)
A plastic carton of the local liqueur flavoured
   with tree bark and fish scales
An inflatable lilo for the swimming pool
A pack of cured meat for which none of your
   translation apps can identify the source
   animal

Your dad will doggedly make his way through this last item during the course of the holiday, insisting that it actually tastes really good as he chews away on it for thirty minutes like it's a discarded piece of car tyre.

What Dad Says: 'I can catch
   up on some reading.'

What Dad Means: 'I will fall asleep after
   every paragraph of this spy thriller.'

Your dad's holiday will quickly fall into a routine once you've done the things every resort holiday requires. These are:

1. Somebody else going on an actual food shopping trip and coming back with food that could realistically be assembled into a meal that humans eat without giving themselves gout within a week.

2. A walkabout to see the sights of the local town. In your dad's head, he will be a cultured traveller casually strolling between the ancient town walls, stopping occasionally to examine an interesting piece of architecture, perusing the wares at a flea market to find some bargain piece of craftsmanship, solemnly enjoying the cool, darkened interior of a church as he takes in the medieval triptychs and iconography. He is wearing a linen suit in this version of himself and can chat easily with passers-by in whatever language they speak. *James Bond: The Retirement Years* just about covers it.

In reality, he will stomp along the hot, narrow pavements at the same pace he uses during his morning commute, shouldering his way through tourists like he's going to miss the 8.15 train if he doesn't get a move on. After five minutes your dad will realise that the streets in a tourist beach town will all have the same things on them:

- Restaurants with people stood outside asking him to join them while handing him a menu the size of a suitcase with photos of the meals printed on them and the descriptions translated into English. They have turned the menu to the English translation page (French, German and Dutch translations also available) because with his bright red forehead, hurried pace and general air of discomfort he could not look more British if he was wearing a T-shirt with a picture of Churchill on it.

- Gift shops selling fridge magnets, bottle openers (which he no longer needs as he has worked out how to open those bottles of beer with a fork and the door handle, using a method that has seen 'sticking plasters' added to the shopping list) and every other imaginable item large enough to print the name of the resort on them. This includes key rings that turn out to be small, carved wooden penises, which he only notices on closer inspection after picking one up to take a look at it and dropping it when he realises what it is.

- Other holiday villas that inevitably look nicer and more centrally located than the place you're staying, which was advertised on the website using pictures that defied the laws of Photoshop and managed to find angles of the rooms that missed out every dangling electrical fixture and mysterious wall stain, as well as hiding the construction site visible out of the kitchen window. The advertised 'five-minute walk from the beach' suggests that previous guests have included Usain Bolt and a family of cheetahs.

· A shop that isn't quite an off-licence, isn't quite an amusement arcade and isn't quite a place where you could probably buy a gun if you knew who to ask, but is somehow an amalgamation of all three and usually has a group of teenagers hanging around outside that your dad pretends not to be absolutely terrified of. This kind of shop is never more than eight feet wide and it never closes, a fact that became apparent during the first night of your stay because it's directly opposite your villa.

3. Establishing a regular pool lounger, bar and restaurant. Your dad is a creature of habit, as the indentation on the sofa at home demonstrates, and while a holiday is a chance for him to shake things up a little, he can only truly relax once he knows what he's going to be doing for the duration of the trip. This also allows him to have a little disingenuous moan on the final day about all the activities he never got round to doing.

Once he finds a pool lounger location that has

the right ratio of direct sunlight, distance from the apartment and distance from the pool bar, and he can reserve without waking up at 5.30 a.m., this will be the pool lounger he will sleep in, face under the paperback with the author's name in embossed gold lettering on the cover, until it's time to go home.

. He will find a bar that has some fellow Brits in it so he can chat to them of an evening, but not so many that there's a risk of it raining plastic chairs if a football team loses a match. He'd prefer it if the staff spoke English, but preferably with a local accent rather than if they were born ten minutes from where you live. UK sports shown quietly on TVs in the background would be great, rather than a twelve-foot projection screen in a pub named after a UK war hero, animal or sitcom.

He'd like to sit outdoors in this bar and see the sea while he has a drink if possible, but not if it means watching shoals of lads stagger past like wheelbarrows full of testosterone and vomit. 'Foreign, but not *too* foreign' is the way he would describe it, but he knows how that sounds and he's really not like that.

And while the resort offers more restaurants than he could possibly visit if he stayed for a month, he will find one in the first couple of days that he likes and will refuse to go anywhere else. The seafood there is really good, he will insist, and they have an interesting selection of local wines that he doesn't drink but he's glad are on offer because it suggests it's not just a tourist trap.

The fact he is a tourist and puts half his holiday money in their till is an irony that is lost on your dad but he's happy, which is the main thing. This is because he ordered a local delicacy on the first night and the waiting staff complimented him on his good taste, choosing to ignore the fact he left three-quarters of it uneaten. Every subsequent night they greet him as 'my friend' or 'boss' and ask if he wants his usual table before escorting him through the largely deserted dining area. They even give him a glass of liqueur for free at the end of the meal. They do this with every dad in the restaurant, but this makes your dad feel special in a way he seldom gets to feel.

Especially when he goes shopping for food when he's on holiday.

The Shed

What Dad Says: 'I think I have
   one of those in the shed.'

What Dad Means: 'I may be gone some time.'

Typical Dad Joke: 'I should get another one
   and you could call me Two-Sheds.'*

To you, a shed is a wooden outbuilding typically found
in the rear garden of a residential property, used for
the storage of items associated with gardening and
building maintenance as well as long-term storage for
non-essential belongings.

   To your dad it is a Mecca, a state of mind, a place
of contemplation, a haven, a birthright, a temple, and
a place to store home brew. A shed is not simply a
shed, just as a boat can be anything from something

* This is a Monty Python** reference.
** Monty Python were a group of comedians who had a sketch
   show*** in the 1970s.
*** Ask your dad.

with two oars that you row across a park lake to HMS *Queen Elizabeth*. There are sheds and there are *sheds* and no two sheds are the same, like snowflakes, fingerprints, and the palms of koala bears (this is why koala bears have never got into committing burglaries, as they have yet to master the art of making gloves and they know they would get caught).

When your parents bought your house, while your mum was asking sensible questions about the nearby schools, if the house had any issues with the roof, and whether any of the walls would wobble if you prodded them too hard, your dad was looking out into the garden towards the shed, making plans.

If the house was shedless (a bizarre state of affairs caused by some mental aberration suffered by the house's current owners), those plans would expand to include what kind of shed he would buy once you moved in, and where the perfect spot for it would be. For your dad, a house is not a building that comes with a shed, a shed is a shrine that comes with a place to store his family and all his other possessions.

Despite all of this, the thought of anything happening to your dad's shed fills him not with a feeling of anxiety but with a perverse sense of excitement he can't quite explain or even admit to himself. It's that same flurry of adrenaline you feel when you're stood near a house of cards your sibling has just painstakingly set up, and the reptilian part of your brain whispers to you that you could just knock it down if you really wanted to and deal with the consequences later.

If your dad's shed burned to the ground – and given the assortment of creosote, bamboo gardening canes and wicker garden furniture it contains, it would burn quicker than an oil rig in July – he would then be allowed to buy a whole new shed, and fill it up with a whole new selection of junk. Sometimes, while preparing a barbecue with knots of newspaper and a blowtorch, you see your dad looking over to his shed with a mad gleam in his eye – like a Mafia foot-soldier eyeing up a restaurant that just renewed their insurance policy.

He loves his family too much to ever abandon his car outside an airport, armed with nothing but his passport and the clothes on his back, to reset the clock on his life. Having another crack at existence without a mortgage, in a country with manual jobs where they don't ask too many questions and there's no extradition treaty, might sound fleetingly appealing, but he's just renewed his gym subscription and he needs to be around in eleven months' time so he can never visit the place and forget to cancel it again. But a whole new shed? Full of whole new stuff? That is just the right level of Clean Slate that could make a dad do something rash. Keep a bucket of water handy the next time there's a heatwave, would be the advice.

Nevertheless, there is a padlock on the door of the shed, which your dad says is there to stop anybody from stealing the treasures contained within (and he's not going to let some stranger have the dark pleasure of burning it down in his absence).

He doesn't explain how society would descend into such a hellscape of deprivation that the only means of survival for the roaming gangs of criminals fighting off starvation would be to climb over a garden wall, wade through a knee-high pile of carpet tiles, jam jars full of assorted screws and half-empty bags of potting compost, all so they could climb back over the wall with a rusting Qualcast Lawnmaster 2000 strapped to their back, to sell for the petrol in the tank like a horticultural remake of *Mad Max*.

The padlock isn't to keep out shirtless tattooed raiders with mohawk haircuts and names like Flymo BangCrazy, it's to keep *you* out. If you want access to a shed, go out and get yourself a job, a house, a family, and a strong desire to escape from them on a regular basis. Landmarks of maturity have to be earned rather than simply handed out, and the key to the padlock to the shed is one of them. It also means, in the unlikely event that somebody needs something that might possibly be in the shed, your dad can use this as an opportunity to have an hour to himself to go and look for it.

What Dad Says: 'I'm going to have a clear-out.'

What Dad Means: 'I want to buy more junk
    and there's no more room in there.'

The leaves turning from green to a deep, rich russet. The first silent midnight flurries of snow from a flat slate sky. The loamy scent of earth and crocus that presages the coming of spring. Your dad slapping his thighs and announcing, 'Right, I suppose that shed isn't going to tidy itself.' These are the things with which we mark the passing of each year.

Once the weather turns decent enough that your dad isn't going to get rain-drenched while he drags out bin bags of what can only be described as 'stuff' from the shed – but not so warm that he will be dripping in sweat after twenty minutes, like that time he signed up to do a 5K charity 'fun' run and needed the St John Ambulance to give him Lucozade and an ice pack – the urge will overtake him to clear out the shed.

In the past, your mum has tried to divert this sudden burst of energy into more worthwhile pursuits like finishing the decorating in the spare room that was started so long ago they don't make that colour of paint anymore, but she may as well hold a hand up to an avalanche and tell it to get back up that Alp. Shed-clearing season is upon us.

Just as items from eBay aren't simply categorised as 'new' or 'used' but are given every gradation between – like 'as new', 'still smells new', 'a bit used but it's 99p what do you expect', 'might have to shake it to get it working', 'it's your funeral if it doesn't work', 'bury it as soon as it arrives' – the stuff in your dad's shed has degrees of usefulness.

Obvious stuff like the aforementioned lawnmower (much coveted by the deadly Strimmer Pirate gang) and barbecue are going to be kept, unless your dad is feeling confident enough that now would be a good time to upgrade something that sits in a damp wooden box all year round, only to get used three or four times at most.

At the other end of the scale, there is the stuff that is definitely going to the tip. Because if there's one thing your dad loves as much as his shed it's taking a carload to the tip. The camaraderie with other tip-visiting dads, the joyful feeling of lobbing things into metal skips the size of his house, getting terse nods of approval from tip staff because he knows the correct tip etiquette and procedure (newer dads are easily identified by how much they have 'THAT'S FOR THE BLUE SKIP NOT THE RED' barked at them, like army recruits at their first day of boot camp), the opportunity to come back with more items than he left with because 'it was only going to get thrown away and there's nothing wrong with it' . . .

If some enterprising soul could build mechanised tunnels from the municipal tip that came up from beneath the floor at the back of dad sheds, creating a never-ending Möbius strip of junk to be categorised, bagged, transported, disposed of and shipped out to another dad to rediscover in another shed many miles away, the happiness levels of dads across the country would skyrocket.

'Look at that, it's a harp with no strings. Don't remember buying that,' some dad would say, breaking down the instrument into easily transported parts with a contented smile on his face. By the time he got back from the tip, the space it occupied would be filled with a box full of Johnny Mathis albums and a rotting kitchen cabinet for him to deal with. Dad heaven on earth could be achieved by somebody with the vision to undertake the biggest infrastructure project since the Victorian sewers, only this time the crap would be flowing in the opposite direction.

Until that happy day, your dad has to make sure his shed has a steady supply of junk for the tip by moving everything in it one rung down on the rank of usefulness. At one end of the scale is the shiny unused drill taking pride of place hanging off a bracket near the door, and at the other end, buried in the corner, is a set of sun loungers blooming with sufficient mould spores to generate a new strain of antibiotics strong enough to tackle the MRSA virus.

At some point in the distant future, when a tech billionaire has built sheds on Mars to house the tools that his army of space slaves use to mine the planet for minerals and you have a thriving shed of your own, your dad will find a rusted lump at the back of his shed, shrug and toss the (still unused) drill into a bin bag so it can be taken to the tip, and the council's nanobots will give him a pre-programmed nod of approval when he throws it into the right skip.

What Dad Says: 'Bit over the top, isn't it?'

What Dad Means: 'I am so consumed with envy I may actually start crying.'

Not all sheds are created equal. Some are no more than shoddy lean-tos created by nailing bits of discarded wood and corrugated iron to the side of the house until there's enough of them to keep some of the rain out, so your dad can store stuff in there so long as he doesn't mind it being permanently damp.

They're home to creatures who scuttle away when

he opens the 'door' (five pieces of mismatched laminate flooring screwed together) that he assures your family are voles, but this doesn't stop him arming himself with a mop from the kitchen whenever he goes inside. He tries to give it a joke name like 'The Conservatory' to detract from the fact the 'voles' have started making their way into the house and are gnawing their way through the wiring.

In the evolutionary scale of sheds, these are Neanderthal constructions, barely worthy of the name 'shed' but sharing enough characteristics with their sophisticated, modern shed relatives to be recognisably part of the same family. Small, dangerous and foul-smelling, they are capable of storing basic tools, but only if you keep them in a waterproof box away from the part of the roof where the two bits of corrugated plastic don't join together properly.

Most sheds fall into the middle category – functional square boxes with bitumen roofing and 'windows' made of Perspex that can be pushed in quicker than it would take for any Shed Raider to look at the six-digit padlock affixed to the door and ask, 'Why don't we just steal this instead? It looks valuable.'

Their walls are painted in a variety of colours from 'decommissioned battleship' grey to 'decommissioned mental hospital wall' blue to 'I'm about to vomit on a car ferry' green. Inside is metal shelving that is largely eschewed for the more traditional storage solution of piling everything on the floor. They smell like a mixture of must, rust, and a level of weedkiller fumes your dad hopes isn't dangerous when inhaled for too long.

These sheds can vary in size from 'fairly roomy coffin' to 'unscrupulous landlord puts a bed in and rents it out'. While Parkinson's law observes that work will expand to fill the time allotted to complete it, the amount of stuff your dad owns will expand to fill the size of shed he owns. Something like the Economy Micro Efficiency model shed might mean your dad can barely afford to possess a shovel and half a dozen used plant pots gained by carefully killing a number of houseplants over a period of months.

But if a Goliath Deluxe Behemoth model were suddenly to materialise in your back garden like an oversized beige Tardis, your dad would instantaneously be the owner of half a ton of scaffolding, the engine from a Nissan Micra, and enough rolls of Astroturf to carpet the whole of Leeds. He would awake from a stupor days after purchasing all these items with absolutely no idea where he got them all from, how much they cost him, and why he thought he needed a crate of forty-seven bowling balls.

Despite the disparity in size, they are all recognisably sheds, in the same way when a Chihuahua sniffs the bottom of a Great Dane, it knows it's another dog that's being sniffed. The increasing scale of sheds traces a line from their primitive beginnings towards the era of enlightenment (indeed, the ability of a shed to contain mains lighting that doesn't kill your dad in a shower of blue sparks is one of the things that marks it apart from its ramshackle ancestors). It shows the shed striding away from the medieval four-walls-and-a-door era of their development into the modern age, where the latest developments in science and technology have stopped their roofs blowing off every autumn.

But what your dad really wants is The Shed Of Tomorrow.

The Shed Of Tomorrow, or TSOT, is not named because of its futuristic design. Indeed, TSOT has been around since the 1970s, when your dad looked at photos of them in magazines* as a kid and wondered whether it would ever sit alongside the jet-powered car and That Singer Off of *Top of the Pops*** as part of his sophisticated adult life.

The Shed Of Tomorrow is so named because it represents an aspirational dream of the future that is tantalisingly possible in a way that flying cars and Kylie

---

* and ** These are both things that used to exist, don't worry too much about it.

Minogue simply aren't, yet is always just out of reach because if he ever suggested building one for himself, the costs involved would see him laughed out of the living room, house and halfway down the street.

TSOT isn't a wooden outbuilding typically found in the rear garden of a residential property, used for the storage of items associated with gardening and building maintenance as well as long-term storage for non-essential belongings.

It's a lifestyle.

It smells of air freshener rather than old wood polish. Your dad would invite Pete to visit rather than store bags of peat in it. And forget a six-digit pad-lock, this shed would have a more sophisticated alarm system than your dad's car.

This is a shed that has a TV in it, and not that 18-inch one from Argos with the cracked screen that fell off the kitchen counter last year. A plasma TV. Your dad has no idea what a plasma TV is, whether you need to buy bottles of plasma to keep it going, or why plasma is a good substance to have in a TV. Your dad is unaware that they don't make plasma TVs anymore, but he still thinks that they are the best ones so that's what he wants, connected to cable TV and Netflix, in TSOT.

The TV will be on the wall behind the bar. The

bar that has an actual beer pump that serves actual chilled beer in actual beer glasses to be placed on actual branded beermats. No more drinking lukewarm supermarket-brand lager stored in the garage straight from the can. This is going to be *classy*.

It will be heated, of course, as there's no point in having a shed that cost more than his first flat if your dad can't sit in it for eight months of the year without wearing a coat. Besides, it has to be heated as he doesn't want all the sports/film/music memorabilia hung on the walls (that were previously consigned to a box in the attic) to get damp. The damp would also play havoc with the felt on the pool table.

The ultimate accolade for The Shed Of Tomorrow your dad builds would be that on opening night (yes, this is a shed that is worthy of having an opening night), that bloke off the telly comes to visit. The one who walks into people's houses and sheds on his show and says, 'Wow, what an amazing space you've created here. Mate, this is brilliant,' and has a bit of a natter and a pint with the owner as the credits roll because they get on with each other so well.

Deep down, your dad knows TSOT will never happen and the closest he will ever get to it in his own shed is playing cards while sat on bags of builder's sand with the feller from next door while they share a four-pack of Guinness. But owning a shed that could be transformed into something magical like TSOT is like owning a lottery ticket before the numbers are drawn. What makes it special is not what it is but what it could be.

Even when it smells like fox pee.

The Boyfriend/Girlfriend

What Dad Says: 'I promise I
won't embarrass you.'

What Dad Means: 'I promise to
put some trousers on.'

Typical Dad Joke: 'Don't do anything I
wouldn't do, which leaves a lot of scope.'

Puberty is an embarrassing time for anybody. Bits of your body suddenly decide to go on a hormonal rampage, doing odd things and growing to odd shapes and sizes. And all that hair. It's like slowly becoming a partial werewolf over a series of months, but instead of prowling a Bavarian village for a bit of shepherd to snack on, you've no idea what pitch your voice will be from one minute to the next or why you've burst into tears because the snack machine is out of Wotsits.

It's a difficult part of your life, which can be made easier with a patient, sensitive and understanding parent at home who is willing to talk about the changes you're going through and won't be squeamish no matter how graphic your questions become.

Unfortunately, you have your dad at home. He really tries, but unlike the hairiness of your armpits or the number of pimples on your forehead, he's never going to change.

This reaches its apex when you decide to bring home your first boyfriend or girlfriend to meet your parents. And you thought you would die from cringe to even get to this point.

Dear God, they noticed me looking at them across the classroom, this is a nightmare.

They're talking to me about something, I've got no idea what they're talking about, is it about tomorrow's home-work or the melting point of boron or who won the Best Supporting Actress Oscar in 1974 or oh no they've stopped talking, they want you to say something back, think of a reply, just stop gawking at them and say something back, stop staring at their mouth, what is WRONG with you, seriously, oh great they've walked off now, well you made a pig's backside of that, didn't you?

I think they want me to kiss them. Do they? I want to kiss them, I know that much. Okay, 'want' is putting it mildly. I know that I would give up the final thirty years of my existence, every penny I ever earn as an adult and the permanent use of my left leg if they just kissed me once, just once. Do I lean in and see if I'm right? If I am, then the rest of my life will just be a footnote, an epilogue to this moment ('They went to some university somewhere, got a job doing something which included finding a cure for some disease and they were later apparently knighted by a monarch, but this was all after Stacy kissed them outside Nando's'). If I'm wrong, I will have to learn the basics of kelp farming from Google because I will sprint from this place to the nearest bus station and make my way to the Outer Hebrides to live out my days in a remote drystone cottage near the water's edge, where the chances of one of their mates bumping into me and shouting 'Alright, snogger?' are minimal.

I farted in front of them. Okay, it was great while it lasted.

All of this has to be endured before you feel comfortable enough in their company to suggest that they come round to your house one evening to meet your family. Of course, you might not see them for a few days after making this suggestion, because you will be very busy sat in your room screaming into a pillow and asking yourself what on earth you were thinking several thousand times.

Not all of your family are a problem. You can impress your other half either by showing your place in the familial pecking order by bullying your younger siblings in front of them, or by acting the role of a loving and supportive older sibling (even if this is a complete fiction and you deleted their entire Minecraft civilisation last week as revenge for them spilling something on your favourite coat) – it depends what kind of girlfriend or boyfriend you've decided you are definitely going to spend the rest of your life with. Because it doesn't matter that they are the first girlfriend or boyfriend you've ever had, they are The One. They are the perfect person for you, and the fact that they just so happened to be born in the same twelve-month window as you, in the same school catchment area, and are equally crap at maths so were dumped into the same remedial class, is a pure coincidence.

Grandparents provide a consistent level of embarrassment shared by all teenagers, and as such don't count towards any potentially awful moments in front of The One. If your nan's false teeth fall out during dinner, or they use that word they don't use in a mean way but hasn't been acceptable in polite company for thirty years, it is cancelled out, because when you go to visit their family, their granddad will probably fall asleep in the middle of a conversation or insist on talking about how vigorous his bowel movements have been recently.

In this respect they're sort of like common denominators in algebraic equations, but you're not aware of that because you're in that remedial maths class where you met the love of your life.

Your main worry is your dad, and there's no way The One is setting foot inside your house until you have briefed him in minute detail about what is expected of him when that day arrives.

What Dad Says: 'I've heard so much about you.'

What Dad Means: 'A year in Guantanamo
  Bay couldn't get my kid to reveal
  any information about you.'

In the same way you would prepare an enclosure you intend to house a gorilla in by making sure there are no open windows or machine guns it could accidentally fire off, and checking to see if it contains mango and there are no toddlers roaming around, you need to prepare the house before The One comes round to visit.

You will accompany The One to your house rather than have them arrive on their own, because you need to prep them when it comes to your dad, apologise profusely in advance for every single thing he's about to say and do, and promise that you are nothing like the rest of your family (despite having the same nose, hair colour, and inability to digest dairy products) and have long suspected you are actually adopted. So you need to make sure the house is as un-embarrassing as possible beforehand.

In years gone by, photo albums were an acute source of terror. Page after page of you in the bath wearing nothing but a bucket on your head, in those early years when you insisted on wearing red wellies for every social occasion up to and including going to bed, and photographic evidence of that fringe when your mum cut your hair. These had to be rounded up from their various hiding places (every dad has been through this as a teenager, and he'll be damned if he's not going to put his kids through the same delicious torture, so they hide them around the house to whip out at a moment's notice) and buried somewhere your dad would never find them, like a six-foot hole in the back garden or inside the laundry basket.

When Tim Berners-Lee invented the internet, he no doubt dreamed of the democratisation of information, nations speaking unto nations, and the globe waking up to how interconnected all of our futures are. What he got was several trillion photos of ladies without any clothing, adverts for fake currency, and cloud-based storage for all of those family albums.

This means that now the photo albums are on the phone in your dad's pocket, and there's no way he's not going to make sure it's switched on, fully charged, and open at the photo app album titled 'History of Trick or Treat Costumes'. Given this, your only option is to take a pair of pliers to the wireless router cable before you leave the house to pick up The One. Your dad still thinks Wi-Fi is essentially a form of witchcraft, so there's no way he'll be able to figure out how to fix it and log back onto the cloud before you return.

Your dad will be told in no uncertain terms what he will be wearing when he greets The One. Trousers are a must, and they cannot be the ones he wears while fixing his car. While you've no intention of letting him take The One on a tour of the garden – you've heard him enthuse about compost too often to allow that mistake – he must be wearing shoes AND socks. They have smell-retardant properties, and more importantly are opaque, so the toenails which resemble the talons of a falcon with poor personal hygiene will be hidden. And a T-shirt that didn't come free with a case of beer would be preferable.

Topics of conversation will be vetted. Nothing about you from more than six months ago will be allowed, because part of growing up is looking back at how you used to talk, dress and behave a few months ago in disbelief that you could have ever been such an enormous dork. When you look in the mirror now, you still tend to see an enormous dork staring back at you, but this is at least a dork-in-progress and not such a massive dork that The One runs screaming from you like their hair is on fire.

Music should be avoided because this will go one of two ways. Either your dad will ask The One if they've ever heard of a mid-1970s prog funk band who released three albums of songs with titles like 'Magnesium Complex Redux' and 'Bilbo's Magic Cakes', and offer to burn them a mix CD when they say they haven't. Or your dad will try to talk to The One about current music, saying that he loves the new Tyler Swift album and thinks that Kendrick Limahl is really dope, before attempting a rap that contains words your dad shouldn't be saying.

Sport, politics, school, films, hobbies, work ambitions, religion, weather, plans for the weekend, his childhood, The One's childhood, house prices, books, current events, video games, holidays, pets, environmentalism and the possibility of life on other planets. If your dad steers clear of all of the above, things should go off without too much trouble.

There has to be A Thing happening when The One visits, otherwise it's just a group of people sat in a room staring at a stranger while your dad tries desperately not to think too much about what you get up to in bus shelters.

A meal is usually a good idea, as long as it isn't so fancy The One might make an exhibition of themselves by eating it wrong or slopping half of it down themselves (you've told your parents they're allergic to spaghetti, just to be on the safe side). And the last thing you want to hear is that the slow-roast shoulder of Persian-spiced lamb needs another two hours before it's ready, so does anyone fancy playing a board game while we wait?

But neither can it be the bog-standard type of meal you eat every other day of the year – you want to make a good impression, and various brown crunchy frozen foods heated in an oven for twenty minutes at 220 degrees is hardly going to make the grade. (Here's a cooking tip – ALL brown crunchy frozen convenience food needs cooking at 220 degrees for twenty minutes. All of it.)

A single-course meal of food that isn't too confusing gives just enough time for you to introduce The One to your dad and the rest of the family, but won't take so long that things start to get awkward. Also, your mouths will be full of food for a lot of the time, and your dad can't spend his entire life up to this point telling you not to speak with your mouth full to renege on his beliefs now, can he?

Once the meal has finished, it's time for The One to say how lovely it was, offer to help with the washing-up (this offer will be refused, because there is a very specific ritual to stacking the dishwasher, and now doesn't seem like the time to spend three hours teaching them what it is), and say that they have to go because they have some wholesome, parent-friendly prior arrangement like studying for an exam or engaging in some form of team sport. You will have coached The One on this ahead of time, because as much as they are the pearl in your oyster and the salt on your chips, their mind does have a habit of wandering – and before you know it they've challenged your dad to some Mario Kart and they're calling him a lucky old turd when he wins.

What Dad Says: 'Would you like a drink?'

What Dad Means: 'I need a drink
to get through this.'

All of the above is very specific to the first time you bring somebody home, so it will be different in the future – after you catch The One texting that person from their remedial History class (they really were quite thick, now you come to think about it) or lying to their mates about what happened in that bus shelter – and you bring home the next One, right?

Not really.

Your dad will always be your dad, and his capacity to embarrass you will remain undimmed with the passing of the years. Indeed, it will be strengthened as his ear hairs grow beyond the scope of the hardiest set of trimmers and his ability to regulate his bodily functions dims like a setting, flatulent sun.

There will come a stage when he concedes that it's entirely possible that at some point in your life it may have come to pass that, through a combination of bad luck, forgetfulness, lack of options, tiredness and carelessness, you may possibly have had sex one time, and that the person responsible for this happening is now sat on his sofa, drinking the good booze set aside for visitors, holding the glass in a hand that has . . . best not to dwell on it, really.

Assuming your dad didn't convert your bedroom into that Man Cave he's always dreamed about as a compromise for not getting his Dream Shed (see 'Sheds') – complete with TV with surround sound, sofa and mini fridge – when you come to visit with the latest One it's likely you will be staying the night there. Your dad will be halfway down the stairs with a duvet and a pillow under his arm for the sofa before he's informed of this and told to grow up.

Unlike the brief, tightly timed visit of the first One, you will have the whole evening for your dad to do his dad best to make you wish you'd run away to that Hebridean kelp-farmer's cottage when you were a teenager.

Adulthood simply broadens the ways in which he can embarrass you when you bring home your latest partner, and pointing out that this One is just the latest in a long line of Ones (even if your dating record matches Mother Teresa's in terms of body count) is a great way to do it.

It will be couched in compliments, of course. 'Thank God you've brought one home that can form whole sentences', 'No ankle tag? This one's a keeper', 'I've nothing against face tattoos, but the last one . . .' will be trotted out even if your ex is an RNLI-volunteering doctor who just had their first novel published. If they eat whatever food is put in front of them, this will also be used as a way to criticise your dating record, conveniently ignoring the satay chicken that required a trip to A&E for your peanut-allergic ex.

A trip to the pub might be suggested as a way to break up the evening and stave off the inevitable bed-time situation. This is like tapdancing blindfolded through a minefield, as the local pub will be full of your dad's friends – none of whom are under the same strict orders as your dad to behave themselves, and all of whom will have fantastic anecdotes not only about you but about your dad, including that time he fell asleep in the gents when there was an offer on shots of Apple Sourz because the bottle was almost out of date.

Your partner will insist on paying for at least one round of drinks. Your dad will refuse. If your part-ner is female, your dad now has an added layer of awkwardness by having to explain that it's not because he doesn't think a woman can buy a round, he's all for women's lib, or is it not called women's lib anymore, he's put his card behind the bar anyway so it's just easier, would she like a glass of wine, or a pint, obviously, women drink pints all the time.

Nobody will drink at the rate they would normally drink if this wasn't a night in the pub with their partner's dad. Your dad is itching to order another drink half an hour after you get there, and by the point you'd normally be six drinks in and perusing the cocktail menu, you've barely finished your first. But neither your dad nor your partner wants anyone to think they're raging alcoholics, so an evening of slow sipping ensues.

But the moment cannot be put off forever, and eventually it will be time to call it a night. If society had a healthy and open attitude towards physical relationships, by 10.30 p.m. your dad would slap his thighs, stand up, shake your One by the hand, tell them to give the headboard a good rattling and promise not to forgo the foreplay, and bid them good night.

As it is, bedtime is approached via a series of gradual yawns, references to what a long journey you had this morning, and that you're wanting to be up early to visit friends you haven't seen in ages and a dozen other euphemisms. Your dad thinks this is because you can't wait to re-enact pages 47–113 of the Kama Sutra in your childhood bedroom, six feet away from the room in which he is praying for sudden-onset deafness.

In truth, you will spend the night cramped together in a child-sized single bed, laughing at the old cartoon posters still stuck to the walls, while your One asks, 'Was Eric joking? Did your dad *really* do that on the pool table last New Year's Eve?'

Brothers & Sisters

What Dad Says: 'It'll be nice to
catch up with everyone.'

What Dad Means: 'Please don't let
us be the worst family.'

Typical Dad Joke: 'You've only got so
many aunts and uncles because we
never had a TV growing up.'

Although you may bicker with your siblings growing up, underneath it all you know that it comes from a place of love, affection, and an understanding that if they ever touch your stuff again they will have their most prized possessions flushed down the toilet.

You are allowed to get your little brother in a head-lock and force them to inhale your fart-infused hand. This is a birthright every bit as sacred as the succession of the monarchy, and should actually be incorporated into future coronations by the Archbishop of Canterbury. You are allowed to read your older sister's

diary and laugh yourself silly at the poetry she's writ-
ten about a lad called Darren who works at the nearby
24-hour garage. Play fights in the garden are allowed
to escalate until your dad invokes the age-old risk of
somebody losing an eye and the battle ceases (or at
least ceases after somebody manages to get one final
rib-dig in when nobody is looking).

But if an outsider threatens any of you, they are
taking on all of you, right down to your eight-year-old
brother who may not look like much of a threat but has
been dishing out well-aimed kicks to the groin since
he was a toddler and has been known to reduce 120-
kilogram rugby-playing grown men to a heap of sobs
and dry heaves with a well-placed size-two.

Some stranger can't just come along and kick your
sister's football into the high branches of a tree without expecting retribution. After all, upsetting her by
doing stuff like that is your job. And if some heartless
girl at school decides to dump your brother in the most
public and humiliating way imaginable, she's going to
find his sister has filled her school locker full of bin
juice before the day is out.

What's right is right.

Once you grow up and move away from home,
the intensity of this bond and the amount of times
you give each other a dead leg while walking along
behind your parents may dwindle, but there's always

an element of that dynamic there. When you meet up again, no matter how many grey hairs you can count between you, there will be a little bit of you that wants to knock over an item of furniture and then point at your sibling when a parent notices it's fallen down. You will always be willing to say they started it, even when old age robs you of the ability to remember what it was they started.

But gradually, once the household has disbanded, your siblings become partial strangers to you, with new lives, new interests, and kids of their own that they have to stop from trying to strangle each other. They become Other Adults with Other Adult concerns, and their existence can be so different from where your life is at any given moment that they can appear utterly alien to you.

The various infinite influences of money, geography, life experience and sheer dumb luck will change them in such subtle ways that you begin to wonder how they could possibly have come from the same pressure-cooker household as you. You remember when they'd cry if you stole the last Malteser. So who on earth is this bearded person pretending to be your brother, asking you about your pension contributions?

This is what your dad is dealing with when the aunties and uncles get together, so show some patience with him. You're looking at the adult who raised you, guided you, and dispensed wisdom to help you blossom into the fully formed person you are now. As far as you're concerned, he's stood in a room with other adults who have a similar amount of gravitas and maturity. Meanwhile, when he looks around the room, he's looking at somebody who once told all his school friends he cuddled a pink toy giraffe in bed until he was fourteen, and somebody else who told him there was a Foot Monster living under his bed and gave him vivid nightmares for a month.

You're not in the same room as him at all.

What Dad Says: 'You're looking well.'

What Dad Means: 'Life isn't wearing you out as quickly as it is me, how is that fair?'

When your dad meets up with his brothers and sisters, it's like looking into the multiverse where other possibilities are playing out before your eyes. It's not like the Hollywood multiverse where half the universe dies because somebody neglected to punch a bad guy at the right moment, or a flagging franchise gets rebooted with the main hero appearing from another dimension, only this time with a beard, denoting he is now evil. It poses much more mundane questions.

What if your dad had studied a bit harder when he

was at school? What if your dad was three inches taller and managed to hang on to all his own teeth? What if your dad had been born a woman with an almost-religious devotion to gin? These are the questions that a family reunion answers.

These occasions usually take place at a formal event like a family wedding or a funeral. This places a set of restrictions on how everybody is going to behave – even the most wayward of aunties is unlikely to turn up wearing flip-flops and flinging a frisbee around at either gathering – so it only really shows up the differences between your dad and his siblings under a very specific set of circumstances.

You're sure that the uncle who makes a point of being loudly sociable with everybody in the room can be a perfectly miserable old sod when he's back in his own house and not wearing a suit (the same black one for both funerals and weddings – he's not David Beckham and he can't afford a wardrobe full of formal attire) while carrying a plastic glass of lukewarm flat lager.

You'd like to be equally sure that your auntie doesn't spend every waking moment telling anybody who will listen that your ex-uncle who now lives in Corfu with a dancer and her Shih Tzu named Tiffany was always a worthless bag of @#!£, before tottering off to have a hearty cry in the toilets, but the expression of weary resignation on the faces of your cousins suggests otherwise.

Everybody is a version of themselves in these circumstances, and your dad is no exception. He talks a little louder than usual, laughs a little more at jokes you know for a fact he doesn't find funny, and shows more interest in your uncle's burgeoning sourdough bread business than NASA scientists would show if a new planet shaped like Pikachu suddenly drifted into view between Mercury and Venus.

He wants to show that he has Done Well For Himself, that he is Really Happy With His Lot and that he is Very Proud Of His Kids. Okay, he called you a drooling imbecile last week when you flattened the battery of your car by leaving the lights on overnight and had to call him at 6 a.m. for a jump start, but they don't need to know this. He will say that work is 'ticking along quite nicely' when asked, suggesting he didn't mean it when he recently said he would cheerfully stuff his boss head-first into the paper shredder if he made him work another weekend. And when he calls your house 'this damp old dung-heap', he clearly means it as a term of affection.

It's not easy for him, as uncles and aunties also present a version of themselves that he has to match his life up against. These include:

Indeterminately Wealthy Aunt: This aunt never turns

up to family events in a car that's more than two years old, but the car is never anything ostentatiously expensive. It will be a medium-sized, metallic-grey model with nothing except the logo on the bonnet to suggest that it cost more than you've earned in your life thus far, and has an engine so powerful that until 2007 it would have made it competitive in the Le Mans 24-Hour Rally.

This aunt does something in finance or property, or perhaps financing property. When asked about her job she will wave away the question with a hand adorned with a watch that has its own insurance policy, saying that it's far too boring to explain. This means either she finds her job genuinely boring or she manages financial portfolios for some of the world's biggest scumbags. You have a vivid memory of visiting her one Christmas and seeing a card signed by a South American general, so that may provide a clue.

She's not exactly rude at these functions – she makes a point of asking your dad how he's getting on and even remembers to nod every twelve seconds when he replies. She doesn't look down on him, either. If she ever dared to do that, your dad might be forced to remind her of the sixth-form football team that counted her as one of their trophies when she was at college.

It's just that you can tell for the entire time she's

at the family event, avoiding the wine being served (she wouldn't wash her car with it, and if you knew how much the paint job cost, neither would you), grimly holding on to the same triangular sandwich she was offered when she arrived in the hope nobody notices she hasn't touched it – or even worse, offers her another one – she's thinking to herself: 'I could be in Dubai right now, but instead I'm in a pub function room just off the A1.'

Fair point, really.

Recently Divorced Uncle: Like your loudly sociable uncle, he wears a black suit – but given it's the same suit he wears for unsuccessful job interviews, court appearances and sleeping on his mate's sofa, it is shinier than your wealthy aunt's car. Unlike your aunt, he gratefully accepts any and all food and drink offered to him, making you suspect the cress in the egg sandwiches is the first fresh vegetable he's eaten in months.

He too will wave away any questions about work, but this is done with references to having irons in the fire, prospects about to come to fruition, projects that look promising, and no mention of the zero-hours bar work that is currently keeping him afloat. The divorce hit him hard, as did your aunt when she found out what he'd been getting up to at work with a colleague, and he has struggled to get back on his feet these last seven or eight years since it happened.

If the universe has a finite amount of luck to hand out to the people living in it, this uncle isn't at the back of the queue – he has never been informed the queue even exists. His ability to back a losing prospect is so reliably consistent, your Wealthy Aunt should employ him as a stock exchange consultant, quickly selling any shares he advises her to buy and vice versa.

You feel sorry for this uncle and want the best for him, but not so much that you let him know you just moved into a house with a spare room, because this would be like leaving open an overflowing rubbish bin in raccoon territory. The last thing you want is a topic of conversation at the next family gathering to be 'that injunction order you had to go to court for'.

He will stay at the family event longer than anybody else, leaving with a carrier bag of whatever buffet is left over, as well as some cans for the journey home.

Fun Aunt: There are two types of Fun Aunt. The genuinely fun kind, who talks to you like an equal rather than a niece or nephew to be patronised, given a pound coin with the promise not to tell your dad, and have your hair ruffled. She will sneak booze into your glass if you're of an age where booze-sneaking is required, but will make sure you don't get so drunk you get caught. If you *do* manage to overdo things, she will invent a plausible excuse as to why you need to go and have a lie-down in a dark room, and she will pop in every half hour to make sure you've not vomited everywhere.

She is scandalously honest about her own private life, knows the filthiest jokes you've ever heard, and smokes like a damp bonfire. Your dad will have to tell you several times to go and talk to the other aunts and uncles because, given the choice, you would spend the whole day getting hammered with her instead. All of your mates have an aching crush on your Fun Aunt and will turn up uninvited to any family occasion if there's a suggestion she might be there.

The other type of Fun Aunt tries to rouse everybody into doing karaoke (at weddings more than funerals; she may be annoying but she's not a lunatic) by performing her rendition of 'Sex Bomb' with all the accompanying actions, and she drags you onto the dancefloor like a farmhand snagging a sheep that needs branding. She describes herself as the life and soul of the party, because nobody else would dream of doing so, and has the unshakeable belief that what every party needs is party games rather than plentiful food, music and her leaving everybody else alone.

Her husband sits quietly in the corner while all this is going on, slowly praying for that ache in his left shoulder to blossom into something more permanent so he can escape having to do the Macarena ever again.

Creepy Uncle: You don't speak to your Creepy Uncle, do you understand? We've talked about this.

What Dad Says: 'Oxford, you say? Good for you.'

What Dad Means: 'I think my kids were dropped on their head as a baby.'

Uncles and aunties will inevitably mean the presence of cousins. Your dad will herd you all together and expect you to have stuff in common by virtue of the fact you share an eighth of the same DNA (although in the case of your genuinely Fun Aunt, that fraction may be as little as zero – she's led quite the life). Your dad holds the belief that a herd of people between the ages of two and twenty-five will get on like a house on fire, rather than set the house on fire to avoid having to speak to each other, despite all evidence to the contrary.

It may be that you get on with your cousins, especially if they live nearby and you see them often enough to have stuff in common like knowing what their names are and so on. But this is more by accident than blood, because if the same parents who produced your dad can produce Creepy Uncle, Wealthy Aunt and others like Yoga Uncle, Scarily Right-Wing Aunt and Drugs Uncle, throwing a bucketful of various DNA into the mix can produce cousins of such dazzling variety that there's no chance you're going to like all of them or even understand half of them.

Your dad would like it if you got on with them, though, because it at least proves he brought up a kid that has enough manners to try to get on with their cousins, even the ones like Prison Cousin, Constantly Pregnant Cousin and Came Back From The Army Different Cousin.

Much as he wants you to socialise with them, your dad just hopes that you don't talk to Got Into Oxford Cousin for too long, because they may start a conversation about Joyce and you will inevitably assume this is an aunt whose name you've forgotten.

The Grandchild

What Dad Says: 'They look just like you.'

What Dad Means: 'All babies look
    identical but I can't say that.'

Typical Dad Joke: 'I love babies but
    I couldn't eat a whole one.'

Your dad wants many things for you. To be happy, of course, just so long as your happiness isn't too loud when you're nearby and isn't the kind of high-profile unusual type of happiness that has the neighbours talking about you.

He wants you to be healthy, as evidenced by the long attritional silences at the childhood dinner table with you both staring defiantly at the uneaten greens sat cooling and congealing on your plate. You both knew they tasted awful, but he was obliged, as you will be one day, to chew through them without grimacing, retching or trying to slip them under the table to the dog. This last tactic would be futile in any case, because not even the dog wants cold boiled spinach.

He wants you to have a better standard of living than the one he grew up with. Those memories that are used as a weapon every time you complain about your life growing up, because you don't know what hardship is like. In his day, water was made out of wood and there was no such thing as computer games; you had to make your own entertainment outdoors with nothing but soil and pebbles to play with. You both know he grew up in a terraced house with central heating and your grandparents have photos on their walls of your dad as a kid smiling from the garden of a Tuscan villa they used to visit on holiday, but his point, he feels, still stands.

But more than anything else in the world, he wants you to give him grandchildren. To a dad, becoming a granddad (or grandfather or gramps or grampa or pops, depending on how old you want to make him feel) is like beating the final-level boss of parenting. It's been a long journey, and there were times he was unsure you would make it through unscathed, but he did it. He's steered you through the choppy waters of childhood, avoided the hidden rocks of your adoles-cence, and outpaced the AK-47-wielding pirates of your early adulthood.

When you place that farting little bundle of joy that

smells of nappy cream and sour milk into his arms, he will have docked the parental ship in a safe harbour and he can spend the rest of his days sat in the dockside café of grandparenthood looking out to sea, shouting out instructions that you're steering your parental boat in the wrong direction and the sails aren't fully secured and in his day they scrubbed *all* the barnacles off the hull but far be it from him to judge.

Announcing to your dad that he is about to ascend to the level of Granddad needs careful planning and consideration for how he will take the news. If you're happily married with a great job and a large enough house to accommodate both the new offspring and your dad when he wants to come and visit, the reaction is likely to be tears, smiles, and a quick trip to buy the nearest thing to champagne the corner shop sells (many are the heads of babies that have been wet with a room-temperature glass of Moldovan fizz with a picture of a tractor on the bottle).

If you casually mention the news as you're about to leave for your Saturday job at Tesco, the only time you're allowed to leave the house because you're currently grounded for getting detention at school, and you have been barred from seeing your partner even after you're not grounded and they get out of the young offenders' unit, the celebrations may be slightly more muted.

There is the temptation to announce it as a surprise,

but you have to bear in mind that whenever you start a sentence with 'Dad, are you sitting down? I have some news', his natural reaction will be to reach into his pocket and mutter, 'God, how much is *this* going to cost me?' as he braces himself for another written-off car or broken boiler in the house you insisted on buying despite his warnings about dry rot and radon gas, the latter of which you thought was unnecessary because the place is electric-only.

A common way to spring the news is to show your dad a copy of the baby scan taken by the midwife. This is not without its risks, because without his reading glasses on you may as well be showing him a bathyscaphe survey of the ocean floor near to the *Titanic*. Even once he puts his glasses on, there is still a chance he will have no idea what he's looking at.

Nobody wants to offend expectant parents by asking whether they're looking at a foot, a head, a set of antlers, or an ultrasound of their lower colon they decided to show you for a bit of a laugh – and your dad is no exception. Write 'ULTRASOUND TAKEN . . .' with the date after it on the top of the photo in clear capital letters, and 'YOU'RE GOING TO BE A GRANDDAD' on the bottom, just to be on the safe side. He may still use this as a chance to remind you how atrocious your handwriting is, but it will get the message across.

What Dad Says: 'So long as it has ten fingers and toes, that's all that matters.'

What Dad Means: 'God I hope it isn't ugly.'

The first thing your dad will ask is whether you are having a boy or a girl, and it cannot be stressed enough that saying 'Yes' will not be found to be amusing unless you're having twins.

For your friends, the issue of the baby's sex is a theoretical passing interest, a simple matter of which congratulations card to buy when the day comes – and to provide guidance on whether to say 'he' or 'she' is the loveliest baby they ever saw when they first visit. This comment should not be seen as a lie just because it's pre-planned, incidentally. It's not even because saying 'Wow, did you keep the receipt? That thing looks like it could scare a hyena off a wildebeest carcass. Better luck next time' tends to make the first visit also the last visit. As mentioned, every single newborn baby looks exactly the same. Hospital wrist tags are cheaper than DNA tests, and maternity wards stay well-stocked with them for a reason. So, when your friend says your kid is the loveliest one they ever saw, they're being sincere because no baby out there looks lovelier. Or even slightly dissimilar.

But for your dad, whether he's going to have a

grandson or granddaughter is vitally important stuff, as his future branches off onto two very different paths depending on the answer. You may take the view that gender roles are terribly outdated, that boys can wear pink and girls play football, that there's no such thing as boys' toys or girls' toys and that your kid is your kid regardless of the gender they're born with or the gender they feel most comfortable with. You may take that view because you're right, and good for you.

But your dad will treat a grandson differently to a granddaughter – not better, not worse, just differently – so you need to come to terms with this. If you doubt it, watch what happens the first time they see your toddler fall over and stand up, having grazed their arm very, very slightly. Your dad will either tell them it's fine, it's just a scratch, they're not a baby anymore, or he will scoop them up in his arms, telling them they'll be okay, their granddad has them now, as the tears inevitably start tumbling out.

I'm not going to say which reaction is which, because you already know.

Another thing to come to terms with is the disparity between how strict your dad is with your kid and your dad was (and still is) with you. The inflexible martinet who ensured that spinach was eaten many years ago has been replaced with a Santa-like figure whose pockets seem to contain an endless supply of sweets, pound coins and toys. Pick him up and shake him by his heels while his grandchildren are around, and you're convinced that a fully functioning tree house with a mountain bike in it might fall out.

'Oh, they're only a kid, leave them alone.' Get used to that phrase, you will be hearing it a lot as your child attempts to operate your Xbox with an ice cream or to give the dog a makeover with a marker pen. Transgressions that would have seen you bouncing a ball in your bedroom like Steve McQueen in *The Great Escape* while you Thought About What You Did will see your dad chuckle indulgently and say that they're such a little rogue as they flush another set of house keys down the toilet.

The strange dichotomy in all this is that you have an Ultimate Weapon in your armoury when raising your kid – a scorched-earth threat that can pull the worst tantrum back from the brink and restore order where once there was chaos.

'Stop that or I'll tell your granddad.'

This has an immediate and powerful effect on your child, as if you just told Frosty the Snowman that Bernie the Blowtorch will hear of this. The link between actions and consequences, previously as abstract a concept to your toddler as bedtime, suddenly pulls into sharp focus. The only risk is that whatever prompted you to invoke I'll Tell Your Granddad is so awful a prospect it triggers a new round of tantrums as they plead with you not to do it.

Only very rarely is this threat carried out. You may have a nuclear warhead in your back pocket, but that doesn't mean you need to throw it around every time you step on a piece of un-tidied Lego. When it *is* deployed, your kid is taken to meet your dad, like a shoplifter up before the magistrate to hear their fate. It's a solemn occasion where your dad will read out the charges made against your kid, giving them the opportunity to confirm whether they are true or not. The inexperienced child will try to deny them, adding 'calling your parents liars' to the charge sheet and only making matters worse.

Once the litany of misdemeanours is confirmed, your dad will let out a sigh. He will shake his head. He may even, if overtaken with a flair for the dramatic, throw up his hands in despair. That such a beloved grandchild could behave in such a way. What is the world coming to? Is all hope lost for the next generation, that they could be mired in naughtiness at so tender an age?

The child is sat on your dad's knee as the grand-dad sentence is delivered. In a quiet voice, tinged with sorrow, he will tell them he's not angry with them. It's far worse than that. He won't punish them, what good would that do? It's just that . . . he's disappointed in them.

You almost feel sorry for them.

When your dad does all of this with his grandkids, whether it's wincing every time he hears your kid's trendy name that sounds like a brand of antiseptic cream, or whipping them up into a frenzy of giggling excitement ten minutes before bedtime, or denying that he ever forced you to eat a morsel of food you didn't want, or agreeing with them that you *can* be a bit of a tit sometimes but you mean well, it is powered by something so raw, so unstoppable, that if you saw it in all its naked ferocity it would take your breath away.

Love.

He loves his grandchildren with an all-encompassing passion that he couldn't hide even if he wanted to, and he would endure any hardship to shield them from a single second of sadness. And that's because – miserable, contradictory, corny, tight-fisted, embarrassing old sod that he is – he loves you just as much.